Real Health
for Real Lives

Ages 10–11

Adrian King
with
Noreen Wetton

Published in 2003 by:
Nelson Thornes Ltd
Delta Place
27 Bath Road
CHELTENHAM
GL53 7TH
United Kingdom

03 04 05 06 07/ 10 9 8 7 6 5 4 3 2 1

A catalogue record for this book is available from the British Library

ISBN 0 7487 6717 7

Illustrations by Stephanie Thelwell. Photograph on page 122 by Giacomo Pirozzi courtesy of UNICEF South Africa
Page make-up and editorial by Lodestone Publishing Limited, lodestonepublishing.com and Hart McLeod, Cambridge

Printed and bound in Croatia by Zrinski

Contents

Introduction

Welcome to *Real Health for Real Lives*, a series of four books to help teachers develop the health, social and emotional well-being of primary school children. The content contributes to the children's development towards Citizenship, as well as focusing strongly on individual health and the importance of maintaining it. The book can be used on its own, or alongside its companion *Health for Life 2* curriculum planner book. Many teachers in primary schools will be aware of these highly successful *Health for Life* curriculum planning guides, which have been revised in a new edition (Nelson Thornes 2000). This book, like the three others in the series for the other primary age ranges, links closely to the planning guides, but can also be used independently. It offers 30 lesson plans, each with two photocopiable activity sheets, some of which are integral parts of the lesson, which are intended to lead teachers into a *way* of thinking about stimulating pupil development. The lesson plans are simple to follow and provide a planned programme, but aim also to help teachers become more adept at sifting and mixing ingredients, and enabling children to taste and respond.

Sets of lessons are grouped under:

Healthy Lifestyles: *Me and looking after myself*
Me, my family and friends
Me, my community and environment

and

Sensitive Issues: *Growing up in a drug-using world*
Keeping myself safe
Me and my relationships.

This way of organising the lessons helps teachers to explore the Healthy Lifestyles topics and materials as a sound basis for moving on to more sensitive issues.

Each lesson follows the same format:

- **lesson title**
- **preparation** – a clear indication of any materials needed, including activity sheets
- **vocabulary** – key words that are used during the lesson
- **skills** - which are introduced, reinforced or extended during the lesson
- **kick start** – a short activity that quickly involves the whole class in the topic or issue central to the lesson
- **activity 1** – the first activity, which develops the theme of the lesson, making use of activity sheet 1 either as an integral part of the teaching or as a reinforcement of the learning
- **extension to activity 1** – suggestions for extending the work, offering insights to consider as a continuation of the lesson or as a follow-up activity, including cross-curricular links

- **activity 2** – a second activity developing and extending the theme or looking at it from a different viewpoint. The second activity sheet is used in the same ways as in activity 1.
- **extension to activity 2**, as in activity 1
- **reflective learning** – an important, implicit element of each lesson to help draw out, crystallise, and value the children's individual learning (*see* paragraph on 'Reflective learning' on page 9)
- **reflect and act** – the final section of each lesson, inviting the children to look back over the learning from the lesson, rounding it off by requiring the children to say how they might put it into practice at school and in other settings, such as home or community.

National Healthy School Standard

Schools that have set themselves the targets within the National Healthy School Standard will find that these four books provide a strong and flexible structure for their PSHE/Citizenship programme. In these books health is seen not as an abstract concept but as rooted in balanced physical and emotional well-being achieved by the children through a set of skills, values and attitudes, and through up-to-date information that they learn to access. Children are challenged to see their own role in being healthy, staying healthy, being positive and confident, and growing more responsible for their own and others' well-being.

How to get the best out of this book

The purpose of these books is to provide a series of starting points and directions, though not to dictate the pace and outcome of each lesson, which will be determined as much by the children's responses as by teachers' insight and knowledge of their children's needs. Children need the support of an attentive and responsive teacher who will visit and re-visit ideas and experiences, issues and options as required. Children display a range of preferred learning styles and this book incorporates many of them: drawing, writing, discussing (as individuals, pairs or as a whole class), role-play, devising scenarios, encouraging reflection and interpersonal communication and understanding. As they become more familiar with interactive styles of teaching, they will respond more quickly to the stimuli offered.

Each lesson is set out as though it will be followed, giving prompts and questions to stimulate thinking and to encourage learning to take place. Suggestions are made for different ways of working – as a class, individually, in pairs and in groups – with illustrated ideas for collecting and recording the children's responses as they arise. However, the class may not always be ready to work through the whole of a prepared activity, or may need longer than one lesson to do so. Be ready to be flexible and to use your knowledge of the children, together with the responses they give, to help you judge pace and relevance. The children may themselves suggest activities by the interest they show in a particular topic or by following a different line of thinking so that a new lesson emerges. In some instances these may even replace the suggested activity.

At the end of the 'first steps' each lesson provides, there should be a clear idea of the content the class has covered, its relationship to the PSHE/Citizenship framework and where subsequent steps might lead. If you now want to continue a track that a lesson has followed, you could look for related material in the curriculum planners in, *Health for Life 8–11*. Here you will find ways of dealing with the relationships between issues, ensuring continuity, and ways of planning your programme with close reference to your knowledge of your own children's stage of development.

Baseline Data and Evaluation

Health for Life also provides a full description of the Draw and Write techniques. These four powerful and revealing investigative tools are offered to help you identify children's perceptions of many of the health topics these books address, and emphasise the contribution children themselves can make to our thinking and their learning. These tools are equally powerful as evaluation strategies. At the end of a series of lessons attending to a particular topic, the draw-and-write tool can be re-applied to gauge the changes and the progress of the children's learning.

Keep in mind the importance of developing the children's **emotional literacy**. As young children grow, their understanding of the world around them and their place in it needs to be matched by increasing competence in understanding the impact of their feelings on their own and others' behaviour. The ability to recognise their feelings, to 'read' other people's feelings and body language, and their ability to describe these in a widening language of emotions is critical to their social competence, and to their mental health and well-being. Opportunities for developing these skills and for sharing their growing competence will be found in this book. In order to support the development of emotional literacy we recommend keeping a class record of the vocabulary of emotions generated as the lessons progress. This could take the form of a large circle drawn on a sheet of paper with entries made as relevant words (and the feelings they describe) crop up in discussion or in the context of class life. It can serve both as a growing record of what the class has identified, and a reference for written work. This home-made circular 'wall chart' might be called the class **Circle of Feelings**. We make reference to this cumulative record in some of the activities.

Self-esteem

Self-esteem, which is so vital for personal commitment to safety and for a positive view of the future, needs continual attention, nourishment and maintenance for it to develop as a deep-rooted belief in each pupil that he or she is valuable, unique and irreplaceable. Children need to be ready to cope with change and misfortune, joy and triumph, stress and despair, expectation and disappointment. They need to feel personally strong, loved and supported to be able to face the world and its people. These four books are full of opportunities for teachers to reinforce the children's belief in themselves.

Start where children are – this is where they themselves will start and it makes sense to join them there. Many of the activities in this book begin with questions to the children or challenges to draw quickly or note down some thoughts. This enables you, the teacher, to discover where they are in their thinking, what they know (or think they know), what they have yet to discover, what they have misinterpreted, and to build on these starting points.

This approach can help you decide what further information, exploration, explanation and new skills are needed, and which attitudes and values to challenge or reinforce. It will also help you to develop and extend the children's vocabulary, making it more specific and focused, widening the language of their emotional and physical health and well-being. The language you use needs to be appropriate and challenging for your class.

Build, but revisit, too. Ask the children or remind them of the last time you raised an issue and suggest they look again at it, in the light of more recent experience and growth, to re-examine its relevance in their lives and further develop their understanding.

The Learning Climate

The *Health for Life* classroom has a distinctive learning climate with a number of characteristics:

Expectation and motivation

Children need to know what to expect, and to be self-motivated learners. Expectations are made clear throughout the activities. The children reflect on their learning and the learning process as part of every lesson, providing them with opportunities for self-evaluation, and the teachers with opportunities for praise and celebration.

Autonomy

Children need to understand that they and others have opinions, ideas or experiences that are unique to them. They need to have the confidence to pursue these individual starting points whether, or not they are shared with those of others. Vital to this is the confidence that it is safe to express themselves, whether they start from a well-formed perspective, or from the other end of the scale – a series of vague or basic questions.

Ground rules

A good way of establishing a positive learning climate is to help the class generate ground rules that outlaw put-downs or disparaging remarks, encourage constructive exchange of differing ideas, and help everyone in the classroom feel happy, safe and confident to learn. This can radically improve the atmosphere and the climate for real learning, whilst helping every pupil to feel safe enough to express their views.

Ground rules are best generated by the class members with the teacher's help through a process of sharing and negotiation. Rules should be simple, few in number, displayed clearly, read, re-read, illustrated and reviewed. There is cause for celebration when a rule can finally be put on one side because everyone knows it and puts it into practice! Ground rules have greater impact where the children are invited to contribute to the discussion of sanctions.

Younger children will need help to understand the meaning and purpose of agreed rules, and may want to discuss or draw-and-write what makes them feel comfortable, what gets in the way, and what rules might help them. Collect and discuss their ideas. They can also specify things they would like others *not* to do, and discuss how they will deal with instances of rule-breaking. For example, 'He says he's sorry and he'll try not to do it again. We will try to help him.'

Older children may be ready to work in pairs or threes to say what behaviours by others make them feel (or impede them from feeling) comfortable and safe enough to speak openly about opinions, feelings and experiences. Pool the ideas and make sure everyone (including you!) is clear about what each rule means and is prepared to keep to them. When everyone is satisfied, make a record big enough to display on the wall. The process of sharing and negotiation can make it easier later on for class members to challenge a broken rule if there is unanimity about its meaning and value at the development stage. If children feel committed to helping each other keep to the rules they have produced, this can help the teacher share some of the responsibility for class control, whilst building the responsibility of the children. Collect ideas on how to respond to breaches of rules.

Reflective learning

An important, implicit element of each lesson is helping draw out, crystallise and value the children's individual learning. You may want to do this before moving on to the final 'Reflect and Act' part of the lesson, or as part of that activity. No two children will learn the same thing from a lesson. Open-ended reviewing questions to the children will invite a range of answers, all of which are valid. Ask: 'Tell me something you've learned from this lesson.' Or: 'How would you describe this lesson to someone who wasn't here today?' Let them share their ideas with a partner before listening to some of their answers as a whole class. In this way they can also learn from each other's learning. Acknowledge all their answers – there are no right or wrong responses – and encourage their free-thinking and association of ideas.

The 'Reflect and Act' section of each lesson gives the children a chance to consider what they have learned and how to apply it or extend it in real situations.

Celebration

Work generated from these lessons can be collected into individual, group or class folders, and can serve as a record of progress. This work can be celebrated, shared with other classes, parents, families and the community. Drawings, activity sheets, vocabulary, Circles of Feelings, etc., can form the nucleus of a display to which children can add other material, pictures (computer-generated or painted), photographs, books, artefacts, etc. In this way the material and the children are accorded high value, and there is a graphic visual reminder of the subject matter explored.

Cross-curricular links

There are clear links between the PSHE/Citizenship curriculum and other subject areas, particularly English. Some of these are shown in a series of correlation charts on the Nelson Thornes website at www.nelsonthornes.com/healthforlife. The links with Citizenship are defined in the framework for PSHE and Citizenship, and the associated QCA Scheme of Work for Citizenship (England). There are also clear links with the range of thinking skills defined in the National Curriculum handbooks. Links also exist with other schemes, such as National Health Schools Standards (NHSS), which can be located at www.wiredforhealth.gov.uk, and the QCA guidance for drug education at www.qca.org.uk/ca/subjects/pshe/drug_alc_tob_ed.asp

Links with other national curriculum schemes, such as Scottish 5–14 Guidelines, the Welsh National Curriculum and the Curriculum for Northern Ireland, are also indicated.

Information on PSHE for teachers in England can be accessed from: www.teachernet.gov.uk/pshe

Guidance for teachers in Scotland can be found at: www.ltscotland.com/guidelines

PSE guidance for teachers in Wales can be found at: www.acac.org.uk/pse_framework/PSE.html

The Northern Ireland Curriculum at Key Stages 1 and 2 can be accessed from: www.ccea.org.uk/curriculum.htm

PSHE/Citizenship

Links between the content of the lessons in this book and the PSHE/Citizenship framework are tabulated to help you plan your work and to suggest links to other curriculum material. The links are not exhaustive and may depend upon how a lesson is conducted – you will be able to make further links with your planned Citizenship programme.

English

There are strong links with the English curriculum. Lessons in this book will often involve combinations of reading, writing, verbal reporting, discussion, debate, justifying or challenging views and developing consensus. Skills such as these are specified at the head of each lesson plan. Teachers will often find links with children's literature in the topics and issues presented in these books. Literacy teaching, through the National Literacy Strategy in England, is developing strong cross-curricular links as literacy asserts its status as a skill pervading all curriculum subjects.

Other subjects

Links between the content of the lessons in this book and the National Science Curriculum (England) have been tabulated. Links may be made with other subjects: for example, issues relating to cultural differences may also be raised in Geography, issues of attitude change can be related to historical development and RE, and the display of collected data can be shown as a Maths/IT topic. Teachers will often create their own links and find others not listed in this book.

In conclusion

Whether you are already using *Health for Life* or meeting it and its approach for the first time, in *Real Health for Real Lives* you will find a wealth of starting points and activities. These are presented in ways that motivate children to develop their understanding of what it means to be and stay healthy, the importance of physical and mental well-being, and the contribution children themselves can make towards their own and each others' development.

① Healthy heart maintenance
Ba-boom!

Preparation/materials

activity sheets 1 and 2
Ask the class to help you to
collect empty cardboard
tubes from kitchen rolls, and
bring them to school for
Activity 1. You need one
between two.

Visit
http://sln.fi.edu/biosci/TOC.biosci.html
or seek another good
information source about
the heart. Remind yourself
about pulse-checking:
Seek, (perhaps from your
local Healthy Schools
partnership) the whereabouts
of a local dietician.

Key words

cardiac
abdomen
pulse-rate
cholesterol
stethoscope
fibre
gluten
mineral
deficiency
dietician

Skills

pulse-taking;
considering the importance
of balancing the diet;
making choices

Kick start

Ask the children where their heart is.

Note variations in thinking! What is their heart doing? How do they know? Could it have stopped? How do they know it hasn't? Does it ever sleep? Ask if they can *feel* their hearts beating (without using their hands). They may not be able to, though some may know about feeling their pulse. Show them the proper way, using fingers rather than thumb (which has its own pulse), on their own wrists or each other's.

Activity 1

Share out the empty cardboard kitchen roll tubes the children have collected. If you have enough (one tube between two pupils) invite them to listen to each other's hearts.

This is how doctors used to listen to hearts! The tube is like a stethoscope. Can they hear the noise? What makes the noise? Why does blood need to be pumped around the body? Any pairs without tubes can 'feel' for their pulse. Show them how to 'take' their pulse, timing half a minute for them and challenging them to multiply counts by 2! Expect various pulse-rates around 90 beats per minute. (Action Sheet 1 can be used for recording.) How much variation is there? Will the results be the same tomorrow? Why do pulse-rates vary from person to person? Discuss these questions.

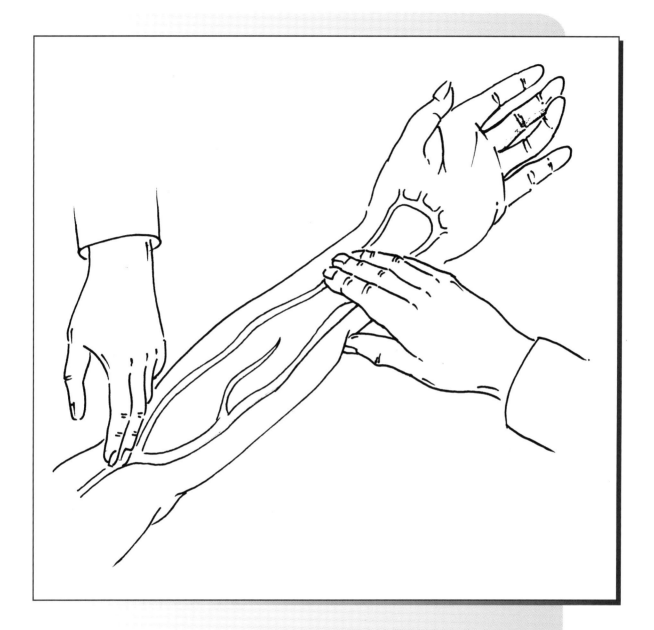

Extension

In an appropriate space, invite the class to do 20 or so jumps or some vigorous running on the spot, until they start to get out of breath. Then ask if they can feel their hearts beating now! (Some may claim to 'hear' their hearts, as their pulse races through their head and ears.) Ask them to take their pulses again, by feel or by tube. Expect faster pulse-rates. Why are their hearts beating faster now? What are the hearts doing this time that is different? Collect and compare these new pulse rates! Can they find ways to represent the class results graphically? (A histogram for the represented rates is one way.) Can they do it on the computer?

① **Healthy heart maintenance** Ba-boom!

Activity 2

Invite the class to talk in huddles and think of all the things that affect their heart's health (stress, exercise, cholesterol, food, alcohol, smoking, etc.).

We know it's good to eat a balance from these food groups:

• bread, cereal, rice and pasta

• vegetables

• fruit and fruit juices

• milk, yoghurt and cheese

• meat, poultry, fish, dry beans, grains, soya, eggs, nuts

• fats, oils and sweets (not too much)

Collect all their suggestions and tell them that today you want to help them take a look at diet. What does diet mean? (The foods we eat, restrictions, instructions.) Talk about diet: why might the doctor put someone on a special diet? Sometimes to get *less* of something, sometimes to get *more* (consider a *high*-fibre diet; a *low*-fat diet; a gluten-*free* diet). Do the children remember in their earlier work the need for balance in a healthy diet?

A heart has to beat about 2.5 billion (2,500,000,000) times in a person's life. It has to be very fit! A balanced diet can help feed the heart, and reduce the chances of problems from too much cholesterol, salt, alcohol or smoking (as well as disease resulting from vitamin or mineral deficiency). Challenge the class to discover how much of the above food groups is healthy and how much is too much, or too little! They can use books, ask at home, or use the internet. Are there any local dieticians they could ask? Encourage and support their information-seeking skills. Collect and discuss their findings! Discourage the idea of bad or forbidden foods. Instead, encourage them to seek balance!

Extension

Mention healthy foods and not-so-healthy foods. (Reserve the term *bad* for food that is old, rotting, mouldy, contaminated, dirty, etc.) What foods are treats? What makes them treats? Ask for examples of food that are best eaten only occasionally (rich, high in saturated fats, expensive, etc.) What happens if they are eaten all the time? (They stop being treats *and* they may unbalance the diet.)

Reflect and act

Remind the children that to help balance their diet, it is helpful to think of more than just the taste of food. Next time there is a choice, ask them to consider whether there is something it would be better to say 'no' to (which otherwise might mean 'too much')? … or 'yes' to (which otherwise might mean 'too little')? Challenge them to make a change for a better balance, and report back to the class!

Lesson 1

Activity Sheet 1 *Ba-boom!*

On this page you can record the speed your heart is beating.
Take your pulse carefully. Then calculate and write down the number of times it beats in one minute.

When my heart is beating normally, it beats _____ times in half a minute.	After vigorous exercise, it beats _____ times in half a minute.
This is a pulse-rate of _____ beats per minute.	This is a pulse-rate of _____ beats per minute.

Your heart has to work very hard for you! Why does it beat?

The purpose of my heart-beat is ....

....

....

....

My heart beats faster after exercise because..

....

....

....

Name _____   **Date** _____

Lesson 1

Activity Sheet 2 *My heart never sleeps!*

Your heart works all the time, even when you are asleep. It beats all your life! It needs looking after, to make sure it can keep on working. Write down some of the ways you can look after it.

To keep my heart healthy, I need to ....

....

....

....

To keep my heart healthy, I try NOT to ....

....

....

....

Draw yourself, doing some of the things that keep your heart healthy!

Look at me looking after my heart!

[drawing box]

(2) What happens when I'm ill?

Ow! Now what?

Preparation/materials

activity sheets 1 and 2
Take note of any pupils
currently with medical
conditions. Be sensitive to
these in the 'health check'
part of the lesson.

Key words

illness
symptoms
malaise
infection
virus
bacteria
trivial
hypochondriac
checklist

Skills

recognising malaise;
reporting unwell feelings;
believing that reporting any
illness is both sensible and
strong;
recognising this strength in
others

Kick start

Ask the class to think of all the reasons why a doctor might be needed (accident, illness, operation, check-up, etc.).

Ask if anyone has seen a doctor because of these things. Listen to some stories, focusing attention on what was 'wrong'.

Activity 1

*Ask the class to tell you who helps people who feel unwell if they **don't** need a doctor (teacher, parent, carer, nurse, self). Who decides if a doctor is needed? (It might be any of these people.) How crucial might the decision be? Discuss this.*

Introduce the idea of a 'health check'. What are the signs and symptoms of a healthy person? Ask the class to get into pairs (or threes) and discuss what headings there could be to a health check they could do on each other. Collect their ideas into a list of health headings.

We could ask about:

sleeping well?   aches and pains   worried about anything?

We could look for:

cuts, bumps, bruises

plasters or bandages

happy expressions

energy and bounce

Ask the children to swap into a different pair or three and conduct the 'health check' on each other, using Activity Sheet 1. Collect the results into an informal 'class health check'.

If the results are more complex, they could be expressed graphically. Discuss how.

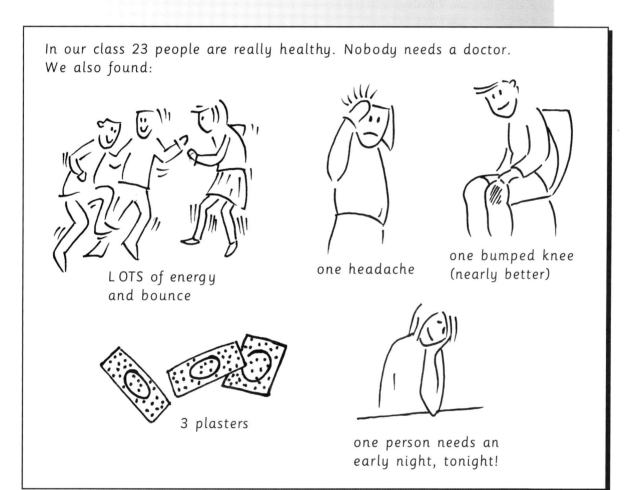

In our class 23 people are really healthy. Nobody needs a doctor. We also found:

LOTS of energy and bounce

one headache

one bumped knee (nearly better)

3 plasters

one person needs an early night, tonight!

② What happens when I'm ill? Ow! Now what?

Ask the class how we can tell when someone is ill? Ask those who drew an unwell person on activity sheet 1 to describe their drawings. Establish the meaning as different from 'out of sorts' or 'had an accident', etc. How do they know when they are ill? When do they first know? Explore their answers and their ideas about early signs. What can cause illness? Discuss this.

Raise the issue of when and whether to tell someone if you don't feel well. Is it good to 'soldier on'? Does it make you a wimp if you rush to tell an adult when you aren't feeling well or you think you may need medical attention? Be ready to explore any gender issues that emerge, and any enduring conditions (allergies, asthma, haemophilia, etc.). Whilst nobody wants hypochondriacs, neither do they want serious symptoms, or progressive conditions (such as meningitis) to go unreported. Try to establish the idea of the children's growing competence in knowing the difference between trivial and serious malaise, and encourage disclosure of anything that might be the latter! Also encourage them to feel it is OK to tell someone even if it isn't serious, or they need some help, or even if they aren't sure. Ask the class to suggest a checklist of criteria to help them decide when to tell someone they don't feel well. After one or two suggestions, ask the children to work in pairs using activity sheet 2. (The feeling stops me concentrating, makes me unhappy, hasn't gone away after 'five more minutes', feel really terrible, feel sick, unwell feeling is getting worse, etc.) Consider displaying the pooled answers.

Extension

In their pairs, ask the children to compose a short dialogue or sketch for two characters. Character A doesn't feel well and, first trying to get full attention, tells Character B who asks questions to find out how the 'patient' feels, and to get a clear idea of where it hurts. Ask for some demonstration performances from brave volunteers!

Reflect and act

Illness can often be treated more effectively if 'caught' early. Tell the children that looking after themselves is very important, and a part of this is reporting when they don't feel well. Say 'Next time you feel unwell, don't wait, tell!'

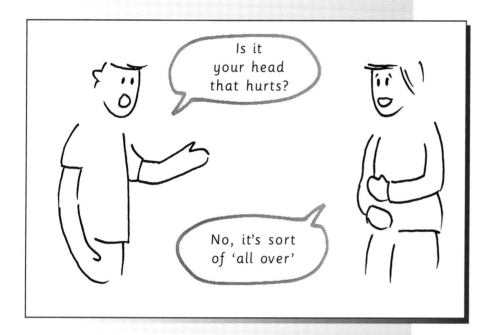

Names _____ **Date** _____

_____

_____

Lesson 2

Activity Sheet I) *Ow! Now what?*

From the class discussion, write down the headings: What to look out for in a health check.

....

....

....

....

....

Record your findings.

We found these signs of good health:

BUT we also found:

Now discuss and agree what a person looks like when they are **not** well. Then agree one of you to draw a speed picture of a person who is unwell. Around your picture you can all write down some of the signs that tell you they are unwell.

This person is unwell and needs attention!

Lesson 2
Activity Sheet **2** *Unwell?*

We think we should always tell an adult that we aren't well, or that we need help, when:

....

....

....

....

....

....

....

....

....

....

....

....

....

....

....

....

We have put a ring round the ones we think are the most important!

③ Health maintenance and body image
Diet for health!

Preparation/materials

activity sheets 1 (one per group) and 2 (one each). Remind yourself of the three main body types: *mesomorph* (android type), *endomorph* (thyroid type) and *ectomorph* (lymphatic type). Check details on a website such as http://www.thefitnesssite.com/bodytype.htm For activity 2, ask the class to bring in some examples of magazines aimed at teenagers.

Key words

nutritious
nutrients
diet
verb: to diet
obese
dietician
attribute

Skills

judging foods for food value as well as taste;
valuing health more than looks, in themselves and others;
recognising that body type cannot be changed and does not by itself determine attractiveness

Kick start

Ask the class to remind you what 'a balanced diet' means.

(Remind them of the work they did in lesson 1.) Ask how the balance is going and how much of the food they eat is *highly* nutritious and how much is eaten more because it tastes nice. Establish 'nutritious' as a variable description – some foods having more food value than others.

Activity 1

Pose the question: 'Is eating a balanced diet the same as dieting?' Ask what the verb 'to diet' means, and for what purposes people diet. Ask the children to work in groups of about four and to use activity sheet 1 to remind themselves and discuss some purposes of dieting.

After a few minutes of huddled discussion, you may find you need to prompt that some diets are to *increase* intake of nutrients, some to *reduce* intake, and some are to help eaters *avoid* something altogether. Why might dieticians suggest each of these? Explore undesirable outcomes from diets, as invited at the bottom of the activity sheet.

Ask how they can discover the food value in (many) packaged foods. Challenge them to find out more about what the terms used on food labels mean and report back to the class.

Do they have any advice for people on diets? Working in groups, challenge them to compile some helpful comments and good advice from their knowledge! (Carefully follow a diet a doctor or dietician suggests; starving yourself can't make you better looking or healthier; a sensible diet isn't meant to make you suffer, it's meant to make you more healthy! etc.)

Activity 2

Introduce the concept of body types which influence the main characteristics of how our bodies look. Judge the amount of detail you need to give to make these types clear, and whether to use their proper names. Discuss the difference between being naturally heavy *and* overweight *(or even* obese*), and* naturally slender *and* underweight *(or even* malnourished*).*

These are the characteristics we appreciate in friends:

friendly manner

no rudeness!

reliable

lend us their things if we're careful

honesty

good sense of humour

likes the same music as us

understands when we're upset

attractive laugh

can keep a secret

puts up with our moods

Ask the class to work in small groups and look at the magazines they have brought in. Challenge them to find examples of all three body types in them (and both genders for each). Ask which type appeared most frequently (ectomorphs? mostly female?). Discuss why this might be. Ask them to browse again and see whether they think any of the female ectomorphs are underweight, and, if so, to suggest reasons for this. Attractiveness is often stereotyped and depicted as purely physical. You may want to use paintings from early last century, such as those by Renoir, Cezanne or Reubens to illustrate that even ideas about physical attractiveness have changed over time.

Establish that it is possible to be healthy and attractive whichever type you are, and that dieting can't turn one type into another; (for example, endomorphs can't diet themselves into ectomorphs and trying to do so can be *very* unhealthy).

In their groups, ask the class to list what characteristics make lasting friendships. How many of these characteristics are physical? What does this tell them?

Extension

Ask the children to use activity sheet 2 to list some foods that could help them maintain their health. Ask them to think of foods they feel they should eat more of, or less of, and any they believe they should avoid altogether (due to allergies, etc.). Remind them that because responsibility for their diet is partly theirs, but shared with parents and carers, they need to discuss diet with them and agree any changes.

Reflect and act

Ask the children to think of a friend (or relation) they really like and the attributes they like in this person. What can be seen just by looking? Perhaps they sometimes see how friendly this person is by their expression. Or see honesty in their eyes. Remind them that diet can't change these things, or create them!

PHOTOCOPIABLE

Lesson 3

Activity Sheet 1 *Diet!*

The word 'diet' can mean more than one thing. Talk about this, and write down some meanings.

We think 'diet' can mean:

....

....

....

Some reasons why a person can have a special diet:

....

....

....

....

....

....

....

These could be the good outcomes of keeping to a diet:

....

....

....

....

....

....

....

Could there be outcomes of a diet that are not so good? Can you say what they are and why this might happen?

....

....

....

Lesson 3
Activity Sheet 2) *Great food!*

Draw some foods you really like. Write the names underneath.

I really like these foods:

In this space write some foods that help you stay healthy. Put a ring round any you think you should eat more of! (Check with your teacher about this if you aren't sure.)

I think these foods help me stay healthy:

....

....

....

....

....

....

List foods that you think you could eat less of to be more healthy! Put a ring round any you shouldn't eat at all (if for example, you have an allergy). Talk to your teacher if you aren't sure.

I think I should eat less of these:

....

....

....

....

....

....

Don't forget: you need to talk to your parents or your carers and agree with them before changing your diet.

(4) Increasing responsibilities

I can manage...

activity sheets 1 and 2
Read through the activities carefully, preparing ideas, resources and special language that may be needed to help the children to be ready for up-coming responsibilities. For example, teachers wishing to use activity 2 as a sex education lesson might prepare opportunities to explore the language needed by children in order to be able to talk about sexual behaviour or sexuality in a polite (public) way when they need to. If catching trains is a current concern, timetables, changing, delays, enquiries, etc. might figure.

Key words

responsible (both 'liable to answer for' and 'dependable')
mortgage
consensus
talent
responsibility (duty, obligation, and the state of being answerable)

Skills

recognising personal responsibility;
discussing; listening;
assisting development of a group consensus;
to understand what it means 'to be responsible', and 'to take on responsibilities'

Kick start

Ask the children to think back to when they first joined the junior (middle) school.

How much have they grown? How much have they grown *up*? How much more responsible are they now? What can they do now that they couldn't before? What do they still need help with? Take examples.

Activity 1

Ask the class if it is just knowledge and skills they need, in order to be capable. What else might be needed? (Age, maturity, height, strength, practice, motivation, etc.)

Explore the 'dependable' meaning of 'responsible'. What does this entail? How might 'responsibility' on occasions conflict with 'freedom'? (Agreeing to run an errand when I'd rather watch TV, helping someone who has slipped over, even though it means getting my trainers dirty, phoning to say I'll be late instead of not bothering, saying no to something I'd like to accept in order to keep my word, etc.)

Explore the children's individual talents. Ask them to work in small groups. Ask the groups to focus on each member in turn, and talk about what they are good at, valuing relationship and communication capabilities, not just academic or physical skills. Give each person a copy of activity sheet 1 and ask them to note one skill on it. Challenge the group to take responsibility for making sure everyone has identified at least one skill. Check no one gets left out! Ask them to note any true talents (natural abilities) in their group, and any conflict between what the group sees and what the individual accepts. Some talented people may need convincing! Establish everyone is, or can become, good at something, but talents are rarer. As a class, celebrate any talents they have recognised.

Healthy Lifestyles 1: Me and looking after myself

Extension

In the Statement of Values at the end of the National Curriculum handbook, one of the statements under the heading 'Self' is "we should 'make responsible use of our talents, rights and opportunities'". Write this on the board and ask the children to discuss in their groups what this means, and what they might do to put it better into practice. Help the class explore whether talented people carry a greater responsibility than others. You could use the biblical parable of the talents (Matthew 25: 14–30) to stimulate the discussion.

Activity 2

Ask the class to call out things they are not considered responsible enough to do yet (buying a house, driving, voting, drinking in a pub, doing the weekly shop, choosing GCSE options, buying their own clothes, picking up their sister from school, etc.). Write them on the board as they are contributed. You may want to suggest some of your own, (perhaps those you prepared) and if the children agree, add them to the list.

Ask them to work in groups and decide which of these responsibilities will arrive or might be needed before they leave school at 16 or 18. Take feedback and underline those they decide fall into this category. Ask them to prioritise, deciding on the top one or two. Criteria could either be 'those that are most important', or 'those they feel they have most to learn about'. If a consensus emerges, start by exploring the top one, helping them identify what they think they need to know, the skills they need to develop or sharpen, how they might get/develop these, and when this might happen. Will this be sufficient to prepare them for this responsibility? Use your prepared ideas/resources as appropriate, to explore or clarify their ideas, questions and needs. (If a consensus hasn't emerged, individuals could work alone or groups could work on an area of common interest. Activity sheet 2 can be used to help them record ideas or questions as they go, for later discussion.)

Extension

Ask the class to reflect on how the issues were suggested, prioritised and discussed. Did everyone feel they had a chance to contribute and be heard? Listen carefully to their answers! Is it only the most popular ideas that should be explored? Challenge them to suggest what you might do to ensure everyone's needs are fairly addressed. Pool and explore suggestions. Point out how responsible they are being!

Reflect and act

Everyone has needs and everyone has responsibilities that change (and grow) as children grow towards adulthood. Remind the children that one responsibility everyone has (adults, too) is to ask when they need to, for information, help or advice.

Name _____ **Date** _____

Lesson 4
Activity Sheet 1) *I can manage...*

Write down one skill you have – something you are good at. (Perhaps your group helped identify this with you.)

I am good at..

....

....

Now draw yourself doing what you're good at. Underneath, write what you're doing. Around your picture, write words that say how you feel when you're doing this.

This is me. I am...

PHOTOCOPIABLE

Lesson 4

Activity Sheet 2) *Soon, soon...!*

(Your teacher will tell you if you will be working on your own or in a group. If you are a group, say 'we' instead of 'I' in the tasks.)

In the box, write the responsibility you want to develop before you leave school.

What do you need to find out, what skills must you develop and what practice might you need?

I will need ....

....

....

....

Think of who *else* will need to consider that you are ready to take this responsibility. How could you demonstrate to them that you are ready?

I can show I am ready to be responsible by ....

....

....

When do you think you might start to make these changes?

I will start to develop this responsibility ....

....

How?
To make this happen, I will need to ....

....

....

(5) Best use of leisure time
That looks fun!

Preparation/materials

activity sheets 1 (one each) and 2 (one per pair)
Read through the suggested activities. (Note: Though they may be unlikely disclosures, be prepared for negative activities (scaring cats, graffiti, glue-sniffing, drinking alcohol, etc.). Be ready to help the class treat them seriously, considering them for what they are, the values that underpin them, the damage or hurt they may cause. Condemning out of hand could be to lose an opportunity to engage constructively with pupils in need.)

Key words

amenities
pursuits
commercial
petition
campaign
councillor
pros and cons

Skills

reflection;
making good use of leisure time;
supporting community action;
widening groups of friends;
trying new activities

Kick start

Ask, 'What did you do at the weekend?' Accept feedback with minimal comment.

Activity 1

Challenge the class to make the longest single list they can, in 10 minutes, of leisure activities they can easily take part in. Ask them first to decide how they will do this. They must end up with a single list for the whole class incorporating everyone's contributions.

The 10 minutes can start only when the strategy is in place and a timekeeper has been appointed! Activity sheet 1 may be of use. (Play in the park, play computer games, watch TV, read, talk to friends, go to the cinema, hang around the shops, go for a nice meal, family activities, etc. Drinking in pubs and watching '18' films not permitted!)

Ask for volunteers to mark the list to draw attention to:

- those that cost money (cinema, swimming pool)

- those that help promote or maintain health (biking, healthy snacks)

- those that are organised specially to include young people (musical instrument lessons, local authority playscheme, after-school club, junior youth club, scouts/guides).

Give each of the volunteers a different coloured pen. Ask each in turn to follow instructions from the class and underline, ring, or star those the class consider to be in 'their' category. Ask them to notice any that have no marks. Is anything wrong with these? Do leisure activities *have* to be health promoting? What if they are risky? Facilitate a discussion to explore the pros and cons of the activities list.

Ask the children to use the lower half of activity sheet 1 to make a note of any from the list that they haven't tried (or done much) before, but might try (again). Ask them to write a reason next to each (looks fun! I need more exercise. James says he'll do it with me.).

Extension

Suggest they share-and-compare their lists with their friends to see if they can gather companion(s) to join them. Perhaps they can suggest time and place, to be confirmed later if parents' permission is needed. It may provide the opportunity for some pupils to make new friends! Supervise plans carefully.

Activity 2

From the list, ask if there are any organised leisure opportunities the children had never heard of before. Ask where they find out about structured opportunities (word of mouth, leaflets, posters, library, internet, live close by, etc.).

Ask them to get into huddles and try to think of a leisure activity that could be organised at school (a play, a club/society, etc.). Each group should have a 'recorder' to write their ideas down, using activity sheet 2.

Take feedback. What ideas do they have? How realistic are they? Could any happen during the school day – perhaps in lunchbreak? Or could a teacher stay after school to help? What might a play be about? Help them explore ideas in groups and as a class, with a view to supporting any emerging initiative(s).

Extension

Is there an activity that they would really like (swimming pool, youth club, etc.) that isn't available locally? Ask if there is anything they could they do about this? Could they travel to the nearest? What about a petition? A community campaign? How do such things work? Tell them every council has a department responsible for local leisure activities. Challenge them to find out the name of their local councillor. Consider supporting them to invite a local councillor from the Leisure Committee into school to talk about their work, and how local people can make suggestions about changes and improvements to local amenities.

Reflect and act

Remind the children that leisure time can be used well, whether it involves commercial, organised or their own informal activities. Being creative with free time can be fun, healthy *and* responsible!

Lesson 5

Activity Sheet I   *Free time!*

Things to do in leisure time include: ....
....
....
....
....
....
....
....
....
....
....

In future, I might	because
....	....
....	....
....	....
....	....
....	....
....	....

Names _____   **Date** _____

_____

_____

Lesson 5
Activity Sheet 2 *New idea!*

Our rough idea for a leisure activity at school:...................................

1 ....

2 ....

3 ....

4 ....

Our best idea is:

....

....

The details are:

....

....

....

....

....

....

....

....

....

....

That looks fun!
Real Health for Real Lives © Adrian King, Noreen Wetton, Nelson Thornes Ltd 2003

(6) My lifestyle
Cool!

Preparation/materials

activity sheets 1 and 2

Key words

lifestyle
harmony
extract
adhere
define
specify
to 'live up to' a reputation
or standard

Skills

self-assessment;
understanding lifestyle;
discussion;
deciding priorities

Kick start

Ask the class: 'What does "lifestyle" mean?'
Write their pooled answers on the board. (Life,
fun, the things you do, food you like, 'wicked'
clothes, etc.)

Activity 1

*What is it about your life that makes up your
lifestyle? On activity sheet 1, invite the children
to draw a speed picture of themselves, and to
write down words and phrases to describe
their lifestyle.*

Cats and jeans are great!   I hate dresses.

I like pop music and vegetarian food.
Me and my friends prefer comedy films.
We go swimming but aren't allowed to ride our bikes out.
I like to visit Gran and help her do her shopping.

(I wear jeans! I'm into rap! I hate junk food! Me and my friends all like reading Harry Potter. I avoid anything to do with football!)

How many different lifestyles are there in our class? Discuss what this might mean. Could there be 28 lifestyles – one for each pupil? Can we identify some groupings in the class who have a shared lifestyle? How could we do this? Encourage the class to find a way to divide into groups who share significant aspects of lifestyle. Assure them the task isn't about whether people are friends or not, just how similar their lifestyles seem to be. If the challenge proves too difficult, explore some of the difficulties it raised.

Extension

What other aspects of lifestyle are there? What about concern for the environment (recycling, using public transport) or being a good citizen, (reporting a fire, or a break-in, helping with the next door neighbour's garden)? Help the class extend their lifestyle horizons. Pursue any ideas which seem to be of particular relevance to the class. e.g. if Citizenship seems to resonate, explore Neighbourhood Watch schemes, keeping an eye out for milk and papers not taken in, etc.

Activity 2

Divide the class into pairs (friendly pairs not random pairs). Give out one activity sheet 2 per pair, and ask them to read the extract which has been adapted from the Statement of Values in the National Curriculum Teacher Handbook. Invite them to choose and specify their three most important statements – three they believe everyone should keep to.

A full copy of the Statement of Values can be found at http://www.nc.uk.net/nc/contents/values.htm

Take some feedback and chair a short class discussion on their views. Is there a class consensus? Ask the children to look back at their lifestyle pictures, and to consider what aspects of their lifestyle are *in harmony* with their chosen statements and whether any aspects are *in collision* with them. By thinking about their lifestyle, can they find ways to change it, to make it more healthy in the widest sense, and to bring it in closer harmony with their most important statements? Invite them to discuss this with each other in their pairs, and to write down any proposals for change.

Extension

There may be some who are ready to tell the class their ideas. Challenge them to turn them into targets! You may need to remind them that a target is one you have to believe you can reach; there has to be a way of knowing you have 'got there'; and setting it has to make you feel good, not depressed or fed-up.

Reflect and act

Remind the children that lifestyle is hard to define! It can be the source of pride, identity and a means of binding friends closely. It can also be a force for good, if the values within it are caring, thoughtful and responsible. Can the children live up to their own important values?

Name _____ **Date** _____

Lesson 6

Activity Sheet 1   *Me and my lifestyle*

Draw yourself. Around the picture, write the words and phrases that describe all aspects of your lifestyle.

This is me!

Names _____   **Date** _____

_____

_____

Lesson 6

Activity Sheet 2 *Good lifestyle or what!*

We value others for **themselves** (not only for what they have or what they can do for us).

We value relationships because they are of basic importance
- ♦ **to us**
- ♦ **to others**

and ♦ **for the good of the community.**

On the basis of these values, we believe we should:
- ♦ respect others, (including people older or younger than us)
- ♦ care for others and be nice to them
- ♦ show others when they are valued
- ♦ earn loyalty, trust and confidence
- ♦ work co-operatively with others
- ♦ respect the privacy and property of others
- ♦ resolve disputes peacefully

Read the statements above carefully. Talk about them in your pair and try to decide and agree which three you think are the most important for *everyone* to try and keep to.
Then write them down here:

We think the three most important are:

1 ....

2 ....

3 ....

We could change these things to make our lifestyles healthier:

....

....

....

....

Cool!
Real Health for Real Lives © Adrian King, Noreen Wetton, Nelson Thornes Ltd 2003

(7) Relationship with relations

Tension!

Preparation/materials

activity sheets 1 and 2
Find a strong piece of string or cord. Prepare it with two harness loops, each big enough for a pupil, like this:

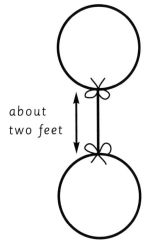

about two feet

Have a short, loose piece about a foot long ready, too.

Key words

relation
relationship
tension
taut
casual

Skills

understanding what they bring to their relationships; appreciating what others bring to relationships; understanding and coping with relationship tensions

Kick start

Ask what makes a relation a relation. (You may choose to 'span' the spread of blood relations and those such as adopted or fostered relationships.) Establish relations as different from friends, but sometimes with an overlap!

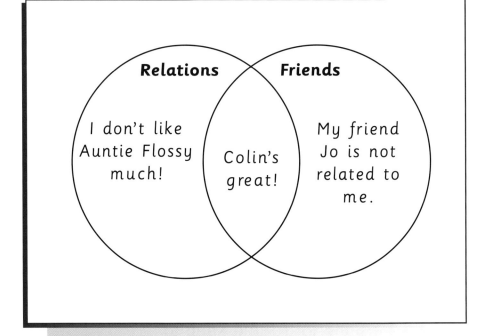

Relations   Friends

I don't like Auntie Flossy much!

Colin's great!

My friend Jo is not related to me.

Ask the children to put up their hands if they have relations they like. (Note any whose hands stay down.)

Activity 1

Explore the difference between 'relation' and 'relationship'. Examine the meanings of 'relationship' as position in family (Dave's a relation. The relationship is he's my cousin) and personal closeness (I have a great relationship with my mate Serena. Jim used to be my best friend last year. Our relationship is more casual now).

Ask the children to think about what they *give* to relationships and what they *receive* from them. Then ask them to consider some examples. Suggest they think of some people with whom they have a good relationship (some could be relations!) and to use activity sheet 1 to write down what they give and receive in these relationships. Establish before they start that you are asking them to reflect on more than just the exchange of cards and presents! (Kylie always cheers me up when I'm miserable. Greg takes me fishing – I do the dishes when she asks me. I listen when he wants to talk about the 'old days'.) In the second box, they will have to imagine what the answers would be. (He'd say he's proud of me. Grandma always gets to kiss me, but I hate it!)

Explore some answers they are ready to share. Are there differences between what one 'gives' and the other 'receives' from a relationship? Why is that…? …and how can we be sure? Explore the value put on relationships, and how different people may value different aspects of the same relationship. 'Giving' can sometimes just be 'putting up with' the other person. (I love my sister, so I let her borrow things even when I don't want her to. Mum puts up with our noise, except when she's on the phone.)

Extension

Pair with a friend. Tell each other one thing you like about him or her, and one thing you put up with because you're friends. (**No** feedback from this one.)

⑦ Relationship with relations Tension!

Think about your family and how you feel about each of them. Has this changed as you've grown? In what ways? What makes them special? Think about the problems you have, too. Is there sometimes tension? Illustrate this with the short piece of string – one person pulls this way, the other person pulls that way (show the string is taut).

Ask for two volunteers. Put one loop of the harness around each and get them to stand so the cord is taut, but their arms are free. Ask each to lean *very slightly* backwards, so that the cord is under tension. Tell the class the length of the cord represents their relationship. It's quite a close one. Say the tension represents a difficulty they have. Ask who they might be (brother and sister, father and son, etc.). What would happen if the cord was under so much tension it broke? (Don't let them try this!) They wouldn't be so close any more. Instead, how could they reduce the tension? (Each would have to 'give' a bit.) Get the pair to demonstrate. Allow a second pair to 'have a go' if enthusiasm indicates a desire. Can the second pair illustrate a different relationship or tension?

Extension

Ask the children to write a little story on activity sheet 2. Two relations have a close relationship, but it's under tension. Ask them to write about the two characters and what caused the tension. Finally, their story should tell how each 'gave' a little, so that the tension was released and they became closer again.

Take some feedback to illustrate a variety of ideas. Remind the class that this illustrates 'resolving disputes peacefully' from the Statement of Values. (Was this value one of the important one the class identified in Lesson 6?)

Reflect and act

Ask the children to think of ways to reduce the tension in the family by giving a little. Remind them that sometimes the relationship is more important than what is causing the tension!

Lesson 7

Activity Sheet 1 *We get on well!*

Think of some people you have good relationships with. You don't have to write down their names. Now write down some of the things you give and receive in these relationships. (Ask your teacher if you aren't sure.)

What I 'give' in my relationships	What I 'receive' from relationships
....	....
....	....
....	....
....	....
....	....
....	....
....	....

Thinking about the same relationships, what would these people say they receive from their relationship with you?

They would say... ....

....

....

....

Is there any difference between what you give, and what they would say they receive from their relationship with you?

PHOTOCOPIABLE

Tension!

Write a story about two relations in a family. There is tension – write about how this started. Write how each one found a way to 'give' a little and move from the position causing the tension. Make your story end happily with a closer relationship and less tension! Illustrate your story, too, if there is room.

My two related characters' names are:

and

Their relationship is: (e.g. mother and daughter)

and

The story:

....

....

....

....

....

....

....

....

....

....

....

Check your spelling and punctuation carefully – how hard have you tried?

Tension!
Real Health for Real Lives © Adrian King, Noreen Wetton, Nelson Thornes Ltd 2003

(8) How does my family 'see' me?

Look over here!

Preparation/materials

activity sheets 1 and 2
Ground rules may need to
be reviewed before this
lesson, to ensure put downs
or other hurtful remarks
are, with the children's full
agreement and co-operation,
outlawed.

Key words

introspective
diligent
thorough
conscientious
meticulous
caring

Skills

summing-up people;
recognising different
perceptions;
accepting others' views of
me;
taking responsibility for
personal change

Kick start

Ask the children to think of some famous people they admire (pop stars, actors, authors, etc.).

As each name is suggested, ask for volunteers to think of a trio of three separate words that sum up the person (rich, gorgeous, talented) (Brazilian, quick, crafty) etc. Accept all reasonable answers! Different ideas will emphasise there is no single right way to sum someone up.

Activity 1

After exhausting the ideas for several celebrities, ask the children each to list four people they know well. Suggest they choose a variety of ages and genders, across friends and family.

Using activity sheet 1, ask them to draw speed pictures of the heads, of their four people in the boxes and underneath each head, write the person's name. (Remind them a speed picture is drawn fast – no marks for art – each is just a quick sketch.) In the space next to each box, ask them to write three, separate words to sum up the person.

Explore how these descriptions might be arrived at. Should the three words describe the person's most important characteristics? or the most noticeable ones? or those qualities for which they are known? or should they reflect aspects which are only seen after being friends for a while? Discuss these ideas as a fair basis for 'summing someone up'.

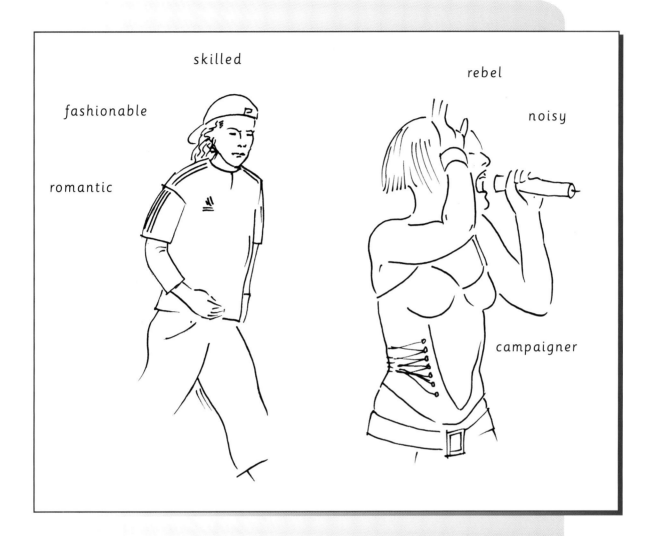

skilled

rebel

fashionable

noisy

romantic

campaigner

Extension

Ask for volunteers to pick one person (not someone from the class) from their worksheet and present them to the class, saying why they have chosen each of their three words. The class can ask them questions about their chosen individual, if they wish.

Activity 2

Ask each child to think of three words or phrases that describe themselves (black, strong, shy; a good laugh, friendly, enthusiastic; skinny, helpful, good at swimming, etc.). Allow a few minutes and then ask for some volunteers to tell the class. Some word trios may be 'higher risk' than others: acknowledge their courage where appropriate. You may want to introduce some of the key words above, or add suitable words or phrases for your class, perhaps by asking: 'If someone described you as ... what would they mean?'

Ask if anyone disagrees with any of the words. Stress that any replacements must be both true and constructive. Take some contributions. Establish that, aside from factual disagreements, people don't always see us as we think they do, or might like them to.

Ask the children to think of their family and to choose one of them; then on activity sheet 2, draw and write how they think this person 'sees' them. Explain what 'sees' means here. Help them consider their expression (sad? happy?) and what they are doing (always watching TV? head in a book? being helpful?). Say: 'How would they describe you? How do they feel about you? Write some words around your picture that they would use about you. Write as many words as you like.'

Then in the next space, ask the children to write down how they would prefer to be described. There is space for them to reflect on the differences.

Extension

Ask the children to think what would need to happen before their chosen family member would be likely to describe them as the preferred words do. Can they make it happen? Would they need to change to be described in this way? Challenge them to make changes into targets! Remind them there are three vital elements to good, personal targets: you have to believe you can reach them; there has to be a way of knowing you have 'got there'; setting them has to make you feel good, not depressed or fed-up.

Gently ensure they know that changes take time to put in place, and it may take considerably longer for them to be noticed. One way to speed up the process of recognition might be to share the target with the person they want to notice the change they are planning. What might they say to this person?

Remind the children that everyone is seen a different way by different people. Is the way they see others fair? Is the way others see them fair? Reinforce that they can't change others, but they can change themselves!

(Lesson 8)

(**Activity Sheet** ⏵ I) *To sum up...*

To draw a speed picture (head only) of four people you know well. Choose a variety of ages, from your friends and family.

Name ....

Write three words that sum up each person.

1 ....

2 ....

3 ....

Name ....

1 ....

2 ....

3 ....

Name ....

1 ....

2 ....

3 ....

Name ....

1 ....

2 ....

3 ....

Name _____ **Date** _____

Lesson 8

Activity Sheet 2 *Look over here!*

1 Think of a member of your family. In the first box, draw yourself how you think this person 'sees' you.

2 Next to it, or round it, write the words you think this person would use to describe you and how they feel about you.

```



```

In this box, write the words you would **like** your chosen person to use to describe you.

> I want my person to describe me in this way: ....
>
> ....
>
> ....
>
> ....

Look at the words you have written in the lower box. Are they different from the words in the first box? If so, why aren't these the words your person would use to describe you?

It's because ....

....

....

....

(9) Recognise and learn from critical situations
Next time, I'll...

Preparation/materials

activity sheets 1 and 2

Key words

waft
conscious
hazard
dependent
fictitious
fortune
scenario

Skills

recognising critical
moments;
judging options and possible
outcomes;
taking greater responsibility
and control

Kick start

Explain that a 'critical moment' is the point where things could go one of two (or more) ways; a point where not just fortune but a conscious decision could change how a situation turns out.

Activity 1

Tell the children the following story-opening: Alex lived in a small house with his mother. It had rained for much of the week, but when Saturday came Alex awoke to find the sun shining. He pushed back his quilt and, still a bit sleepy, threw on his jeans and sweatshirt, pushed his feet loosely into his trainers, and then quickly brushed his hair. The delicious smell of breakfast was wafting up from downstairs. Halfway down the stairs, Alex glanced out of the window and...

Ask, 'What happened next?' There are no right answers. What did he see? A friend? A bird? A car? Did he wave or call out? Perhaps he fell. Did he trip on his laces? Or on a book left on the stairs? What the children suggest depends both on their imagination and their experience. If the story turns out well, it doesn't mean the hazard might not have been there. If Alex does fall, does he break anything – a picture off the wall? his arm? Emphasise that any of the possibilities *might* have happened, but nobody knows which.

Ask the children if there was a critical moment for Alex in this story. Perhaps they think there was (pushing feet into trainers; Alex's glance) or perhaps not (just a succession of events leading to the outcome).

Extension

Ask if the children can give you examples of critical moments from their own experience. What options were there? Which did they choose? What made (or helped) them decide what they did at the critical moment? Can they recall accidents where they made the wrong decision? or didn't recognise the moment? or didn't think? How important do they think it is to recognise critical moments?

Activity 2

Ask the children to write a short scene that has a clear critical moment in it, and an outcome beyond. They may choose either to work alone and recount a real event, or, if they cannot think of a real example, work with another person to make up a fictitious situation. The scenario must be realistic (not an adventure story) and its outcome must depend on two things: a) recognising the critical moment and b) deciding what to do. Happy endings are fine, particularly if they really happened!

Invite volunteer author(s) to read out their stories. Some may involve accidents and other unavoidable predicaments or mishaps, so while you help the class explore each, focus particularly on stories where you judge worthwhile learning may ensue. Challenge the class to pinpoint the (most) critical moment in each story, to say what decision was made, to suggest an alternative decision and how that would have changed the outcome. Ask the children to think carefully about how realistic it would have been to expect the character to foresee the alternatives and to decide on a sensible course of action. Use 'What if…?' to extend their thinking. Ask what 'traps' they think might get in the way of careful thinking at critical moments (temptation, impetuousness, bravado, enthusiasm, other strong feeling). Can they suggest how to get round each of these traps?

Extension

Invite the class to tell you what they have learned from this lesson. Can they identify something from their learning that might change how they act in the future? Discourage simplistic notions of right versus wrong, sensible versus silly, accident versus safe. Instead, challenge them to be realistic in how they might apply their learning to situations where they have some control.

Remind them that it's much easier to be wise after a mishap, but noticing critical moments and avoiding problems is a skill worth developing!

Reflect and act

Explain to the children that analysing everything they do is not possible! But recognising critical moments can be very valuable, along with prompt, careful thought and action at these significant times.

Name _____ **Date** _____

Lesson 9
Activity Sheet 1 *Look out Alex!*

Draw a scene from Alex's story. It may illustrate a moment from the story-opening your teacher read out to you, or you may choose to draw what happened later.

This is Alex.

Names _____   **Date** _____

_____

_____

(Lesson 9)

(**Activity Sheet** 2) *Critical!*

Write about an event that includes a critical moment. Try to make it a real one. Be careful to describe the critical moment, the decision that was made, and the outcome. (You may have time to illustrate your story on the back.)

The character(s)

....

....

....

The situation

....

....

....

The critical moment was

....

....

The outcomes

....

....

We think the character(s) could learn this (from what happened):

....

....

....

Next time, I'll...

Real Health for Real Lives © Adrian King, Noreen Wetton, Nelson Thornes Ltd 2003

(10) Coping with moods
Leave me alone!

activity sheets 1 and 2

Key words

humour
moody
depression
gloomy
blues
strategy

Skills

recognising 'low' moods in
self and others;
knowing how to cope with
their own such moods;
having options for offering
support to others

Kick start

Ask the class: 'Show me how you're feeling today!'

Comment on this bright, happy-looking bunch, but remind them that not everyone feels good all the time. If any are demonstrating a not-so-good mood, show some sympathy at an appropriate level.

Activity 1

Ask the children what emotion they feel when they've just fallen over and grazed their knee (upset, frightened, shocked), or have missed a bus (angry, frustrated), or when a sports event (local? on TV?) has the wrong outcome (disappointed, let down).

Challenge the class to draw a picture of themselves when nothing particular has happened, but they are, the same, just 'not in a very good humour', out-of-sorts, moody. If they don't feel like that now, can they recall the last time they did? Ask them to draw their picture on Activity Sheet 1 and to write around it words to say how they feel and, if they can, what causes them to have feelings like these.

Show the class some of the pictures if the artists agree, and focus briefly, in turn, on the words describing their mood, and the cause(s). Invite sympathetic responses from the class if relevant! Add any new words to the class Circle of Feelings.

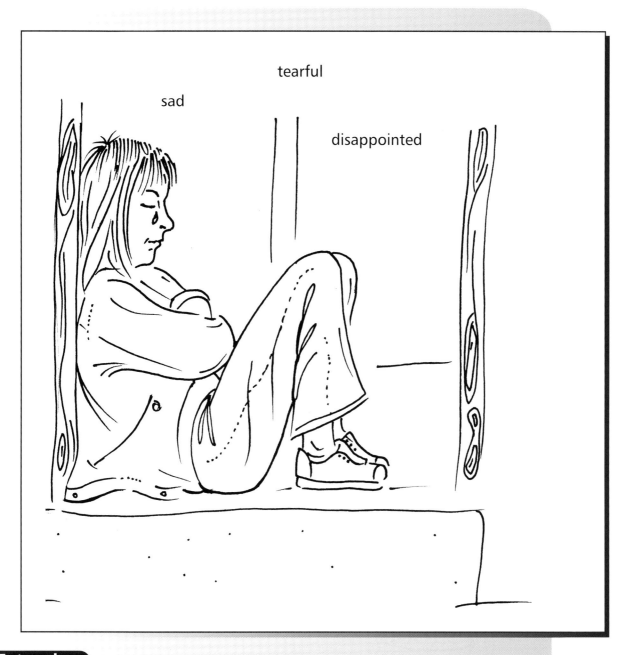

sad

tearful

disappointed

Extension

Ask for volunteers to say what they do to help manage an uncomfortable mood.
(I kick a football; I sit quietly; I talk to my cat/teddy/hamster; I take it out on my
little brother). Suggest they work in small groups, and pool their ideas about what
to do on activity sheet 2. Remind them different ideas will work for different people!

Some strategies have cons as well as pros (my little brother tells my Mum; people
get cross when I don't answer them). Invite the children to discuss their ideas.

⑩ Coping with moods Leave me alone!

Activity 2

Can they compose some helpful advice to moody people?

Ask the class what this advice might need to cover. Write their suggestions on the board. (taking time out; expressing their feelings e.g. to cat or on football; seeking sympathy and support; avoiding upsetting others; addressing the cause, with help if needed, etc.)

Ask the children to return to working in their groups and to discuss what advice they might offer any glum friends. Ideas can be recorded on activity sheet 2.

If your friends are in a gloomy mood, how can you help? Ask them if they've ever asked someone who looked a bit down or miserable 'What's the matter?' and been told 'Nothing!' Ask them what 'nothing' means in this case. (Leave me alone! None of your business! Don't want to talk about it! I can't put it into words!) Is there another way to express concern without saying 'What's the matter?' Ask them to consider this in their groups and make a note of any ideas they generate on activity sheet 2.

Extension

Ask the class to reflect back to a time when they felt 'down', or downright miserable. Ask if any can recall how their friends supported them – can they say what a friend (or relation, or teacher) did that helped them? Ask for examples of what has helped. There won't be one right answer that fits all, so the children may learn from the variety of helpful things that friends have done (left me alone, gave me a hug, listened, showed they cared by asking what was wrong, invited me to his house to play with his dog, was 'there' for me). Ask if they would like to make a class display of helping options! If they do, suggest they each draw an example, with a caption. Show it off in assembly!

Remind the children that when sad or quiet moods happen, it's good to have friends to rely on. If a friend (or relation) looks miserable, show them they matter – put some of the class strategies they have learned to work!

Name _____ **Date** _____

Lesson 10

Activity Sheet 1) *Not so good, today...*

Draw a speed picture of yourself when you feel out-of-sorts. Around your picture, write some words to say how you feel. If you can, also write what makes you feel this way.

This is me when I feel 'down'.

Leave me alone!
Real Health for Real Lives © Adrian King, Noreen Wetton, Nelson Thornes Ltd 2003

Names _____ **Date** _____

_____

_____

Lesson 10

Activity Sheet 2

Some ways to manage moods

The moody person could...	But this might happen...
....	....
....	....
....	....
....	....

Advice to anyone feeling 'down'

1 ....

2 ....

3 ....

4 ....

5 ....

6 ....

When a friend looks out-of-sorts, you could try saying:

....

....

....

....

⑪ What friendship is
Mates

activity sheets 1 and 2
Think how you can get your class into groups so that it splits their common groupings. A random split could do it (form a line according to birthday, and then allocate A, B, C, D, E, etc. along the line). Or are they responsible enough to split *themselves* up if the clear instruction is given?

Key words

summon
loyalty

Skills

being able to judge what binds a friendship group; experiencing and starting to assess group dynamics; knowing the importance of 'belonging' to a group for themselves and for others

Kick start

Ask the children to think of a time when a friend 'stuck by' them. Take some examples. Then invite them to reflect on a time when they stuck by a friend. Can they describe some of these situations?

What does it mean to 'stick by' someone? Does it always mean to do what they want? (Suppose they need help but are afraid to ask, and they beg you not to tell – are you sticking by them if you summon the help they need?)

Activity 1

Ask the class: what makes people become friends? (Because they like each other; because they live next door to each other; because they both like computer games.) Why do people stay friends? What is the 'glue' that makes them 'stick' together as friends? (Values, activities, likes.)

Arrange the class into groups of children who don't normally work together, dividing 'tables' and other usual friendship groups. You might choose to make the groups random. Ask each group to think about an imaginary group of friends, and in discussion to decide:

● how many there are in this imaginary group (big? small? does it change size? how?)

● what activities this group are usually involved in (organised? casual? usually the same? changing?)

● all the things that make the group 'stick' together (think the same way? admired 'leader'? shared interest? habit?)

● how the members feel about belonging to this group (wanted? 'someone'? all feel the same?)

There are spaces on activity sheet 1 for each group to record their thoughts. The space 'But sometimes…' is provided for the group to answer some of the questions in brackets, above.

Extension

Do groups sometimes split up completely and stop meeting or being together? Why does this happen? Has it ever happened to you? How did you feel?

Activity 2

Ask each group to think about how they have worked together during this lesson. Have they worked well? What (or who) helped them to work as a group? If they didn't work so well, why was that?

Ray and Zak argued a bit. We didn't listen to Zena enough. Talking all at once! very quiet! impatient! We could have been more patient with each other. We agreed in the end.

Encourage them to explore these ideas in their groups, picking out some examples of behaviour that seemed to help or hinder effective relations and working, and to relate these to how groups of friends interact. Assure them that if they *don't* feel that they worked well, they have not 'failed'. Perhaps it just means they aren't naturally a friendship group! On activity sheet 2, ask them to draw their (real!) group working together, and, round their picture, to write some of the words that describe how they worked together.

Extension

Do any of the groups have the makings of a true friendship group? (What could their activities be? and their 'glue'?) Or do all the members already have their own friendship groups? Does anyone in the class feel left out – and could they be invited to join an established friendship group?

Reflect and act

Remind the children that friends are really important and belonging to a group can be important, too. Next time they are in their friendship group, ask each other how open they are as a group. Is there anyone who would like to join in? Can they let them? Welcome them?

Lesson 11

Activity Sheet 1 *Mates*

Our imaginary group has ___ people in it. Their activities include:

....

....

....

....

The reasons they stay together are:

....

....

....

....

Some members' feelings are:

....

....

....

....

There may be other things you want to say about the group.

But sometimes

....

....

....

....

(turn over if you need more space)

Mates
Real Health for Real Lives © Adrian King, Noreen Wetton, Nelson Thornes Ltd 2003

Lesson 11
Activity Sheet 2 *Mates*

Draw a picture of your REAL group – the people sitting at your table. Round it, write some words to say how you have worked as a group in this lesson.

This is our group working together..

⑫ Who we love, hate
Friend or foe?

activity sheets 1 (one each) and 2 (one per group) Identify examples of historical and recent/current group hatred (Northern Ireland sectarianism, racial hatred, etc.) with thoughtful reference to the feelings and needs of your class. The lesson invites exploration of irrational hatred, contrasting it with the class ground rules. Take care to avoid upsetting or worrying pupils by spotlighting areas of personal hurt or problems where there are not yet adequate answers.

Key words

genre
universal
recount
associate
valid
entire

Skills

recognising rational and irrational dislikes; tolerance

Kick start

Ask the class to help you finish these sentences in any way they like, but not about individual people.

I love… (ice cream, chips, Blackburn Rovers, *Home and Away*). I hate… (shopping, Mondays, tidying my room).

Activity 1

Ask the children to focus on music. Suggest that it can often be easier to say what *you do or don't like about something, than to say* why *you like or dislike it.*

In pairs or small groups, ask the children to talk about *why* they think some music is popular and some not. Pool and discuss their views. Point out that some people like one pop group, or *genre*, while others will have a different favourite. Some will 'love to hate' a group or singer, even a really popular one – establish that personal taste is an important factor in popularity! Why do some records flop, while others are universally popular? (Some are cool, excellent, people buy them; some are naff, rubbish, nobody buys them.) Is it fair to criticise an entire genre without listening to it? (Classical, jazz, folk, blues, etc.) Why do they think people might do this?

Extension

Now invite the children to think about people and to write down on activity sheet 1 words and phrases they associate with 'loving' or 'hating' a person (admire, enjoy, amazing, friendly, cool, wicked; don't like, angry, hurt, horrible). Take some feedback and discuss briefly. With reference to the class Circle of Feelings look at the intensity of 'Dislike' and the forms it takes from mild (don't really like, don't have much in common with) to strong (detest, loathe). How strong is 'hate'? Do they feel this strongly about anyone

We like Busted!

We like Linkin' Park

We like Kylie

they know? Explore their responses a little. If they detest someone, there's generally a reason – something they have said or done. Establish whether this is the case without probing for details.

Activity 2

Challenge the children to think about this question: is it possible to dislike someone you don't know and haven't met? Ask for examples. If they struggle, ask them to think about supporters of football teams. Some supporters dislike the opposition's fans simply because of the team they support.

Illustrate further with suitable examples from history, such as religious persecution (attacking people because of their beliefs), hunting witches (attacking people because of fear of their powers) or wars (attacking people because of the country where they were born and live). Challenge the children to think of similarities to dismissing jazz or folk, without listening to them. Extend this to other categorical dismissals-without-trying (eating vegetables, reading romantic stories, visiting museums, etc.).

Can the children suggest current examples of group hatred? (Racism, religious sectarianism, political action by minorities.) Help them to understand the word *irrational* in this context: *having no valid, clear reason*. Why do some people dismiss, dislike or even hate an entire group of people without knowing them? (fear, threat, mythical belief, rumour, lies, etc.) Ask the children to work in a group and to discuss this question, drawing and writing their ideas on activity sheet 2.

Extension

Show the children the class ground rules and ask them which rule (or rules) are being broken by people demonstrating irrational group hatred. Would the class ground rules be good for society and for whole countries? Refer to the adapted Statement of Values (Lesson 6, activity sheet 2) Ask which of these values are being broken by irrational group hatred. Emphasise that Human Rights and UK laws are there to put good, workable rules and values in place to protect everyone's rights and needs! Do the children have any advice for irrational haters? Listen to their ideas.

Reflect and act

Remind the children that tolerance and acceptance are key elements of school life. But they need not stop at the school gates! If *enough* people practise these values in their lives, irrational hatred could disappear altogether. Spread the *word* – but don't forget the *action*.

Name _____ **Date** _____

Lesson 12
Activity Sheet (I) *Friend or foe?*

'Love' and 'hate' can mean many things. Write down some of the words you mean when you say 'I love...' and 'I hate...'.

These are the words I associate with love:

....

....

....

....

....

....

....

....

These are the words I associate with hate:

....

....

....

....

....

....

....

....

Friend or foe?
Real Health for Real Lives © Adrian King, Noreen Wetton, Nelson Thornes Ltd 2003

Names _____ **Date** _____

_____

_____

Lesson 12

Activity Sheet 2) *Friend or foe?*

Some people dismiss, dislike or even hate a whole group of people without knowing them. What reasons can your group think of to explain this? Draw and write your ideas here.

Our group thought it could be because:

....

....

....

....

....

....

....

....

....

....

....

....

....

....

....

....

....

(13) People who are 'different'
Challenged

Preparation/materials

activity sheets 1 and 2

Sensitivity warning

Be mindful of specific aspects of difference among your class to which they may be sensitive when discussing shared and unique characteristics.

Key words

unique
role
impairment

Skills

valuing difference;
recognising a variety of contributions to groups and relationships;
understanding the feelings of others;
sensitivity to others

Kick start

Challenge the class to generate two lists, the first consisting of characteristics the whole class shares (two legs, a beating heart, a member of this class, a bed to sleep in, breakfast this morning) and the second of characteristics unique to each (name, likes and dislikes, fingerprints, face, personality).

Activity 1

Each child in this class is unique. Everyone is! Ask the children to list which of their personal characteristics will change as they get older (height, tastes, responsibilities, boys' voices, girls' breasts, etc.) and which will probably remain (colour of eyes and skin, beating heart, talents, disabilities). Discuss whether there could be any exceptions in this latter list.

Return to the unique attributes each child has. Collect and write on the board examples including the general (name, voice, skin colour, gender, etc.) and the specific (short-sight, hearing impairment, etc.). Invite the children to think of uniqueness in their *behaviour*. Does someone in your friendship group say 'Let's…' ? What name could they give this person? (Ideas person, initiator.) Does someone else say 'What if…?' (Guard, caretaker.) What other roles are there in the friendship group? (Timekeeper; Provider.) Ask the children to work in groups and think about their own and other friendship groups, and to draw and write down roles and talents of which they are aware on activity sheet 1. Give each their own sheet.

Extension

Take feedback and compare the variety of perspectives and experiences. Seek the children's recognition that lasting groups often depend upon a variety of 'members' whose roles, talents, attributes and personalities are all different.

⑬ People who are 'different' Challenged

Activity 2

Set the following scene:

A group of friends were together in the playground. Their break was not due to end for a while. One of the group suddenly said, 'I know, why don't we...' and outlined her idea.

Another said, 'We could ask Gina to help, she's good at it!'

'Oh, no, she won't want to join in – she's not like us.' (Of course, the scene might refer to Mike rather than Gina, but the story is the same.)

Ask the children to work in groups to address some questions based on this scenario:

1 What could the idea have been (during school time? later?) and how did they know Gina was good at it?

2 In what way was Gina 'not like' the group? (shy, low confidence, in a wheelchair)

3 Put yourself in Gina's shoes. How might she feel to be excluded in the way that was suggested in the story?

4 Might it be right – that Gina wouldn't want to join in – and how could the group have found out for sure?

5 Can you describe some traps you think the group were falling into?

6 Thinking about the discussions in activity 1 of this lesson (about friendship groups, roles, personalities and talents), what advice do you have for the group?

Discuss their answers, showing sensitivity to actual relationships in the class.

Extension

Suggest the children extend the story on activity sheet 2, to include more dialogue, and an outcome. Some may simply want to engineer a happy ending. Others may be more ready to make the verbal interchanges significant and revealing, maybe not reaching full agreement and resolution within the fictitious group. Perhaps the playground break ends before there is time to approach Gina! If there is time, spotlight and explore some ideas from the finished stories, using 'What if…?' where appropriate to extend their thinking.

Reflect and act

Remind the children that everyone is different and everyone has rights, needs, feelings and abilities. Can they find new ways to include those around them the way they like to be included? Encourage them to discuss this with their friends!

Name _____ **Date** _____

Lesson 13
Activity Sheet 1 *Challenged*

Think of what groups of friends do together. Does everyone like the same things? Who decides? How do you stay safe? Who watches for traffic or other hazards? What other 'jobs' are there? Draw people from friendship groups and write about their roles next to them.

Lesson 13
Activity Sheet 2 — *Challenged*

Continue the story of the group and Gina (giving her or any other characters suitable names). What else do people in the group say? Is there a disagreement? Is Gina part of the discussion? Can the story please everyone? How does it end? Write your story here and illustrate it over the page. You may want to choose a title after you have finished writing.

My title for the story is: ....

....

....

....

....

....

....

....

....

....

....

....

....

....

Check your spelling and punctuation
carefully – how hard have you tried? ....

Turn over to illustrate your story...

Challenged
Real Health for Real Lives © Adrian King, Noreen Wetton, Nelson Thornes Ltd 2003

(14) Talking intimately about me
Can I whisper?

Preparation/materials

activity sheets 1 and 2
Get hold of a copy of Not
Now, Bernard ! (by David
McKee, pub. Random House
ISBN: 009972541X). It is
excellent for illustrating to
the class the importance of
communicating about their
'monster' problems.

Key words

confide
familiar
trust
persist

Skills

choosing who to talk to;
speaking assertively;
persistence;
plucking up courage

Kick start

Ask the class for examples of 'monsters'. They will suggest fictitious ones. Have they seen the film 'Monsters, Inc'?

Gently lead them to imaginary monsters (the dark, fears, dreams) and those that are real for some people (being bullied, an operation, losing something valued).

Activity 1

Ask the children to suggest some situations (up to six) in which they might need to talk quietly to a trusted person. Here are some possibilities:

Give each situation a number to help the class organise their answers. Give all the children activity sheet 1. It asks who they *could* talk to in these situations, but provides space to say why this might not be easy, they don't need to complete all six if the situations or the person they might speak to are too similar. After a while, take feedback – but tell the children you only want to talk about the communication difficulties, NOT the person they could talk to, nor any problem they might talk about with that person. Stipulate that they refer to 'my person' rather than 'my Mum', to enable you to focus on the *nature* of communication problems, rather than on specific pupils or people. What gets in the way of confiding? Difficulties may be practical (getting attention, finding the right moment, plucking up courage, etc.) or verbal – (what to say, how to explain it clearly, how to stress its importance, etc.). Illustrate using Bernard's difficulties if you need to!

Discuss suitable solutions. Activity 2 focuses on these difficulties in detail.

Extension

Invite the class to reflect on their 'but...' entries on activity sheet 1. How important do they think the personality of the person they might speak to is? and the relationship they have with that person? and how busy he or she is? Their task is to find a way of starting which will work in all situations. Ask them to suggest examples of the opening sentence they might use when wanting to talk seriously to their chosen friend or relative. They may need time to discuss this first, in pairs or groups. Focus on a selection of their suggestions, exploring how effective these might be, particularly in cases where they anticipate some difficulty gaining attention or establishing seriousness.

⑭ Talking intimately about me Can I whisper?

Activity 2

Ask the class to think of three situations: first, where there is a problem getting attention from a chosen person; second, where a problem might be hard to explain; and a third where a lot of courage may be needed before saying what is wrong.

Write suggestions on the board, refining until each has two characters (the one with the problem, and the person they want to speak to) and a clearly outlined 'monster' to talk about. Divide the class into small groups, asking each group to choose one of the scenarios and explore how it might start. (It won't matter if not all three are represented or balance between the three is uneven.) Let them know you accept some groups may engineer positive outcomes, while others may be more pessimistic. They may make notes on activity sheet 2. Encourage realism, not drama! Allow volunteers to illustrate their scenes by acting them out for the class.

Discuss what is presented, focusing not on the 'monster' but on the effectiveness of the character in getting attention, explaining the difficulty or worry clearly, or showing courage in speaking, and the realism of the ensuing scenario. If you don't conduct the extension, you may still decide to ask for (or offer) further options or sources of help for these fictitious characters. Be sure to give the children an opportunity to say how they feel and what they have learned from this lesson.

Extension

Ask the children to work in groups and to pool their knowledge of any *professional* sources of help that can be accessed free of charge. Find out what they know about *local* services (counselling services, Social Services, information shop, well-woman clinics, GP surgeries, telephone helplines, etc.) and national services (national helplines, websites, *national* agencies, etc.). Check for both accuracy and understanding, promoting any of particular or current relevance.

Reflect and act

Remind the children that telling a trusted person about something important can feel hard. Keeping quiet about it can be worse! Their teachers are always there to help, and may be able to sort problems out, or suggest some next steps.

Lesson 14

Activity Sheet 1) *Can I whisper?*

Sometimes, people need to confide in someone they trust. A worry, a secret, a question – they may have to pluck up courage, and choose the right person and a good moment.

Look at the situations displayed in the class. In the spaces, write who you could talk to if something like this happened. (There may be more spaces than you need.)

If you think it might **not** be straightforward to talk to this person, explain why, in the space after the word *but*...

In a situation like No.1   but... ....

I know I could talk to...   ....

....

In a situation like No.2   but... ....

I know I could talk to...   ....

....

In a situation like No.3   but... ....

I know I could talk to...   ....

....

In a situation like No.4   but... ....

I know I could talk to...   ....

....

In a situation like No.5   but... ....

I know I could talk to...   ....

....

In a situation like No.6   but... ....

I know I could talk to...   ....

....

Names _____ **Date** _____

_____

_____

Lesson 14
Activity Sheet 2 *Can I whisper?*

On this sheet, one person from the group can write notes to help you remember.

• the situation ....

....

....

• the characters ....

....

....

• what makes it difficult for one character to tell the other (trusted) character what is wrong ....

....

....

and lastly

• what your group is going to suggest, try or advise ....

....

....

....

....

....

(15) Living in my neighbourhood
Where we hang out

activity sheets 1 and 2: one per group. This lesson is ostensibly about welcoming a new child to the school (and the class) but it is also a device for helping the class consider (and value) the locality, its characteristics and its facilities. Decide where you want the emphasis of this lesson to be: for example 'pride in our neighbourhood' or producing an induction strategy and pack, which the school could use whenever needed. Note the strong links between a 'welcome' strategy and the National Healthy School Standard. Some leaflets publicising local amenities and transport could be useful.

Key words

empathy
apprehensive
defiant
amenities
upkeep

Skills

empathy;
sensitivity;
offering support

Kick start

Does anyone remember being 'new' to this school, or to a club or group, like cub-scouts, brownie-guides, church, synagogue or mosque? Any recent experiences?

Ask what words come to mind when they think about how they felt when they were 'new'. Write some of these words on the board. Did any of the children feel welcomed? What happened to make them feel that way?

Activity 1

Ask the children to imagine that they have just moved to this area, and will be arriving at this school next Monday morning for the first time. How might they feel before they arrive? (Excited, fearful, nervous, apprehensive, curious, defiant.) Add any new words to those already on the board.

The new challenge for the class is to use these imaginable feelings as their starting point for producing a 'Welcoming Package' for a pupil arriving mid-term. Split the class into groups, to discuss and note on activity sheet 1 what could be done to make sure the young person goes home feeling good – welcomed, valued and 'at home'. Their suggestions could be a mixture of *personal* ideas (things someone could do) and *material* ideas (something that might be handed or shown to the new classmate). Help the class to think how to avoid making the 'new' person feel overwhelmed or embarrassed by too much attention. The spotlight can sometimes be an uncomfortable place!

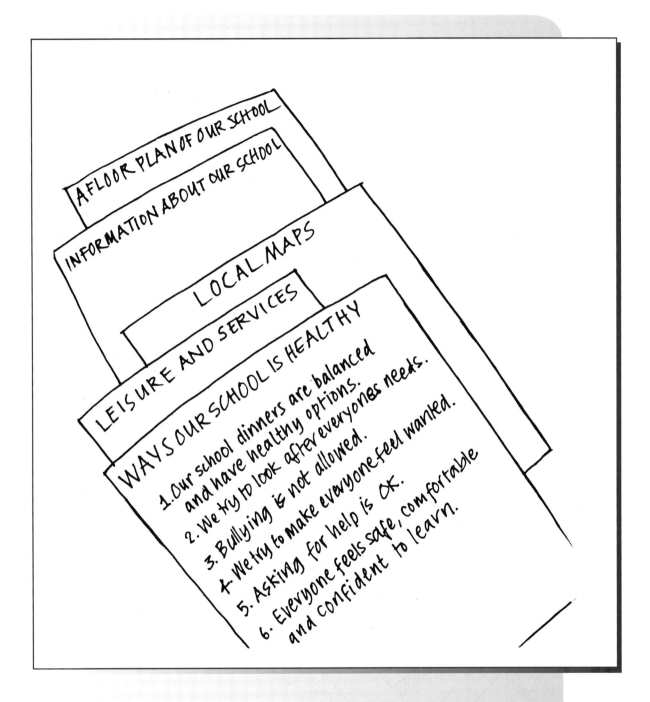

A FLOOR PLAN OF OUR SCHOOL

INFORMATION ABOUT OUR SCHOOL

LOCAL MAPS

LEISURE AND SERVICES

WAYS OUR SCHOOL IS HEALTHY

1. Our school dinners are balanced and have healthy options.
2. We try to look after everyones needs.
3. Bullying is not allowed.
4. We try to make everyone feel wanted.
5. Asking for help is OK.
6. Everyone feels safe, comfortable and confident to learn.

Extension

Pool and pursue their ideas for dealing with familiarisation within the school – tasks 1–4 on activity sheet 1. How realistic are their ideas? Who could take responsibility for these things? How would it be decided? Where would it be written down for convenient use elsewhere in the school?

Activity 2

Invite the class to return to question 5, and ask themselves the question 'What would someone who lived locally need to know?' (Location of library, swimming pool, community resources, shops, bus stops, bus numbers, etc.)

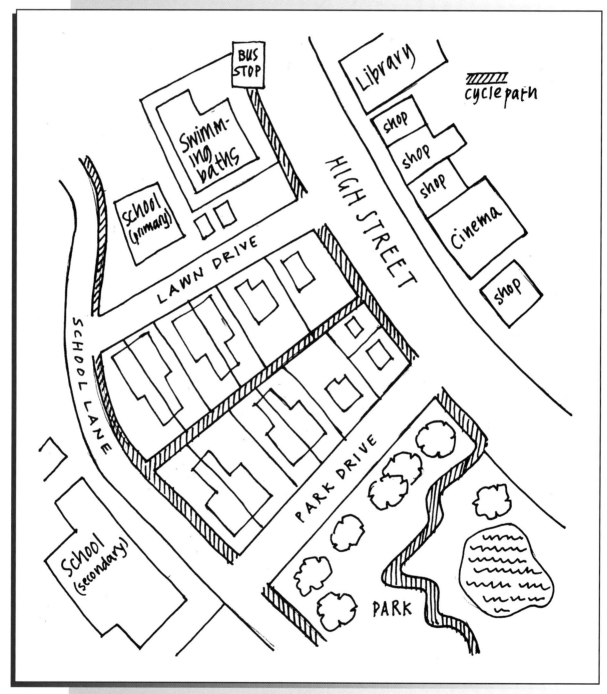

How might they convey this information? (Leaflets, map, 'useful information fact sheet'.) Suggest the task be split for smaller groups to attend to. Some might draft a factsheet, others might rough out a map, perhaps starting from one taken from the internet. Use the school postcode and http://www.multimap.com. Others could do some local research.

Extension

Ask how lucky any new classmate would be to come to our school. And how lucky should they feel about living in this neighbourhood? What are the good things? Where are its special places? Who are its special people? Who is responsible for upkeep and social amenities? What cultures are represented, and how? What needs improvement locally, or greater care, or change? Ask for ideas of how to celebrate our neighbourhood and to promote its 'health' as a good place to live.

Back in groups, ask the children to think of ways in which the local area might be improved. They can record ideas on activity sheet 2. Are some of their ideas suitable for they themselves to act upon? Might they enlist help from others in the school? Might some targets be turned into plans?

Reflect and act

Remind the children that a place reflects the people who live in it. If it is clean, tidy and well looked after, it is because someone has done those things! If not, there is a task for someone. The challenge for the children in class is to find things they can do – and to do them, maybe as a group. Can other classes help too?

Lesson 15
Activity Sheet 1 · _Welcome!_

Your task is to suggest ways in which you, your class, and the school, could make the new person feel welcomed and 'at home'.

1 To make our new friend welcome, we could

....

....

2 To help us all get to know each other, we could

....

....

3 To help the person understand what our school day is like, how we do things, and the class ground rules, we could

....

....

4 To help the person get to know their way around the school, we could

....

....

5 To help our new classmate to become familiar with the local area, we could

....

....

Where we hang out
Real Health for Real Lives © Adrian King, Noreen Wetton, Nelson Thornes Ltd 2003

Names _____ **Date** _____

Lesson 15

Activity Sheet 2   *Where we hang out*

On this sheet, write down some ideas for improving or maintaining the quality of the local environment. In the second column, write down who you think could be responsible for doing these things. For some, it will not be you!

These are the tasks we have thought of	The person we think is responsible is

For the tasks where we think we could take responsibility, this is what we plan to do

....

....

....

....

....

Real Health for Real Lives © Adrian King, Noreen Wetton, Nelson Thornes Ltd 2003

(16) Community groups
On today's agenda...

Preparation/materials

Action sheets 1 (one per group) and 2 (one each). For activity 2, consider which local voluntary, community and pressure groups may be of value for the class to explore, by virtue of interesting role, good example of structure, age and groupings represented in their membership, closeness to school, etc. Your local Council for Voluntary Services (CVS) can tell you what groups exist and how to contact them.

Key words

agenda
pressure-group
community action
gripe
shared responsibility
liaison

Skills

considering need for change;
negotiation;
campaigning;
self-expression;
making alliances;
taking charge;
acting responsibly

Kick start

Ask the class to consider in pairs what could be done (by them or others) to improve the school environment, or the 'working' of the school.

Collect their ideas and encourage action which each individual can take (being more polite, better punctuality, quieter behaviour when appropriate, working harder, etc.). Then focus on those ideas where group effort (or persuasion of those with power/responsibility) may be needed. Establish that for these, one person is not enough!

Activity 1

Next, pursue one or more ideas ripe for 'community action' which could be purely internal to the school (recycling more, taking a greater part in planning assemblies, re-organising where books are placed in the school library, cultivating a neglected area of ground, putting on a school play with staff involvement, etc.).

Don't dismiss unrealistic ideas at this stage. Try to end up with a short list of favoured ideas for strategic planning and action. Split the class into groups of four or five, giving each the task of drawing up a 'plan of campaign' for one idea. You may choose to use activity sheet 1 for this. If there are several distinct ideas, share them out among the groups keenest to address each; otherwise, let each group try to generate the best strategies for the chosen idea. If necessary, help each group consider how realistic their idea is, what they could do, whose help or co-operation they might need, when they could start, how long their plans might take, etc. Boosting recycling, for instance, might need carefully thought-out ideas, the help of head teacher and staff, co-operation of parents and the children in other classes, information and advice from Friends of the Earth and liaison with the local authority, and might easily take a couple of months or more to put in place.

Extension

Suggest each group makes a pictorial representation of their idea, showing the steps, and the successful outcome. Encourage a separate illustration for each manageable step. Judge carefully whether use of a computer might help or hinder your class' purposes and needs, here. Display these pictorial plans in the class – they can act as progress charts as action takes place and can also be used to help recruit collaborators from elsewhere in the school!

Activity 2

Explain to the class that groups exist in the community – groups of volunteers who share an idea, vision, interest, need or sometimes a gripe, and get together to do something about it.

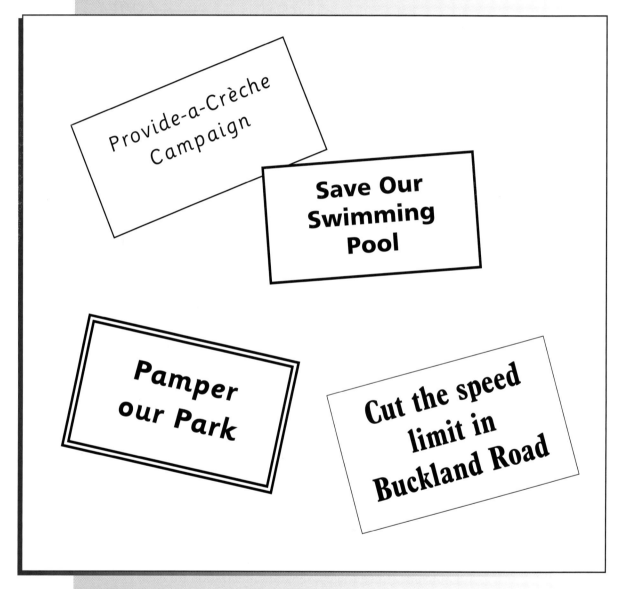

Provide-a-Crèche Campaign

Save Our Swimming Pool

Pamper our Park

Cut the speed limit in Buckland Road

Illustrate with information about some local examples. Explore with them the difference between interest groups (aerobics, line-dancing, quilting) and campaigning groups ('Provide-a-Crèche Campaign', reduce the local speed limits, renovate the park play-area, 'Save Our Swimming Pool'). Ask if anyone knows where to find out about local groups. (Internet, library, ask teacher or at home, look at school notice board!) What about starting one – how could this be done? Draw on their own ideas and experiences from activity 1. Chair a discussion to explore possibilities.

Extension

Suggest, using your local knowledge, that the class might like to meet someone from a local group. Would they like to invite a visitor? If so, help them contribute to a letter of invitation. (Who should actually write and sign it – a class representative? a group?) The class could use activity sheet 2 to note things they would like to find out (how did the group start? what is it for? how big is the group? what difficulties does it face? how can we help? etc.) and the things they learn when the visit takes place.

Reflect and act

Explain to the children that the efforts of a group can be more effective than those of one person, or people working separately. Complaining is easy, but doesn't often get results! Taking considered action as a group can be better at raising an issue or bringing about change. Can they see anything that needs to change locally? Does it need a campaign? Is there one already that needs more support?

Names _____/_____   **Date** _____

_____/_____

_____/_____

(Lesson 16)
(Activity Sheet) 1) *A plan of campaign!*

Your task is to suggest a series of steps to make your idea happen – a strategy. What must happen first? Who needs to be involved? How will you get the help you need? What do you plan to happen after that?

This is the idea we are working on:

....

....

We think we may need help from:

....

....

These are the steps in our plan:

1 ....

2 ....

3 ....

4 ....

5 ....

6 ....

Time scale. Write down how long you think your strategy will take.

We think our strategy may take

....

....

Real Health for Real Lives © Adrian King, Noreen Wetton, Nelson Thornes Ltd 2003

Name _____ **Date** _____

Lesson 16
Activity Sheet 2 *A visitor!*

Write down some of the things you would like to find out from your visitor.

....

....

....

....

....

Here is a space to write down some of the things your visitor says, and what you find out when you and the class ask questions!

....

....

....

....

....

....

....

....

....

....

....

On today's agenda...
Real Health for Real Lives © Adrian King, Noreen Wetton, Nelson Thornes Ltd 2003

⒄ Emotionally healthy class
It's great in our school!

Preparation/materials

activity sheets 1 (one each) and 2 (one per group).
If your school is part of a local programme supporting progress towards the National Healthy School Standard (NHSS), you will need a copy of the school's list of priorities and progress to date. Familiarity with your local Healthy School Programme (or 'Award') will also be useful in any case. This lesson focuses on emotional well-being, but could be adapted for other NHSS themes.
To find nationally available information, visit: www.wiredforhealth.gov.uk and click 'teachers'.

Key words

emotional well-being
trust
confidential
confide
support

Skills

considering others' needs;
seeking and giving support;
taking responsibility

Kick start

If the children are familiar with movement towards a more healthy school, ask them to remind you what they know about how the school is improving and its future plans. Prompt if necessary! How do they think the school is getting on?

If they are unfamiliar with the concept of a 'healthy school', ask them to talk in small groups about what a healthy school looks and feels like to those inside it. (Their work in lesson 16 may help, too.) Invite them to share their ideas with you, both about 'health', and what makes a school a healthy place.

Activity 1

Tell the children that one aspect of a healthy school, is that everyone should feel comfortable, safe and confident to learn.

This lesson provides a chance for them to explore what helps, or gets in the way, of these safe, confident feelings, but doesn't put anyone 'in the spotlight' with pressure to talk openly about their own bad experiences.

Ask each person to draw two pictures – one of them having a good day at school, and the other showing them having a bad day at school – on activity sheet 1. Around each, invite them to write words that describe how they feel in the picture. Let them know that they will only be asked to show the *pictures* to one other person in the room – someone they trust – but that the two groups of *words* will be collected together as a class exercise.

Extension

When the pictures are ready, invite them to talk to someone they trust, to tell them what is happening in each picture and to swap over when you tell them so that each has a turn. (Be sensitive to these pairings, don't insist on personal sharing unless they can assure you trust exists. If not, invite them to talk generally about good and bad days.) When both have talked about their pictures, ask them to discuss and to write in the space below them what could be done to make the good days more common, and the bad days less likely.

Activity 2

Collect examples of 'good day feelings' from random places in the room and write this collection on a large sheet of paper. Ask for examples of what generates these feelings. Do the same with the 'bad day feelings', swiftly so that attention does not dwell on the givers for long. Write these on another sheet (but avoid probing into what causes these feelings).

Ask the class to consider this second group. How strongly do feelings like this get in the way of learning? Are they 'healthy' feelings to have in school? Is it possible to get rid of them entirely? (Probably not!) Elicit from the class the idea that sometimes feelings like this will happen, but what is important is addressing the *causes*, to reduce the incidence of these feelings, and to support the *people* to try to make sure the feelings do not last longer than they have to.

Ask the children to tell you their ideas about what action can be taken – putting them into categories such as: things that children in the class can do, things you the teacher can do, things that the whole school has to try to do – to maximise good feelings and minimise discomfort or misery. (Could any of their suggestions turn bad days into good days?)

Challenge them to turn their ideas into commitments! For the things that need the help of others in the school, can they begin a campaign to bring them to wider attention? Pursue their ideas to try to make them realistic and concrete, and turn them into plans for real change for a healthier class and a healthier school.

Collect their pictures into two piles: those they don't mind you seeing, and those you promise to destroy without looking at. Check if either group would like to keep them, (or get them back after you've seen them).

Extension

Arrange for small groups to work together. Using activity sheet 2, challenge the children to design an assembly to bring what they have learned, and their intended action, to the attention of the rest of the school. Can they persuade others in the class or the school to join them and to bring about change? Can they set an example to the younger children? Can they use this opportunity to convince everyone that this is a truly healthy class? Explore their ideas, and use them to plan an assembly conducted by your class.

Reflect and act

Remind the children that if anyone feels bullied, frightened, worried or lonely, there is no need to wait for a lesson like this to respond. Make 'a healthier classroom, a healthier school' a target for every day. Invite the children to ask themselves what they can do, and who they can talk to, to make this happen when it needs to.

Name _____ **Date** _____

Lesson 17
Activity Sheet ❙ *Good day, bad day...*

Draw yourself at school having a good day. Write some feeling words around it.

```
Me – a good day at school
```

Now draw yourself at school again, this time having a bad day. Write some feeling words around this one too.

```
Me – a bad day at school
```

What can be done to encourage the feelings in the top picture, and to discourage the bad feelings? Who needs to do these things?

....

....

....

....

It's great in our school!
Real Health for Real Lives © Adrian King, Noreen Wetton, Nelson Thornes Ltd 2003

Names _____   **Date** _____

_____

_____

Lesson 17

Activity Sheet **2** *Assembly!*

Write down what your group has learned so far from today's lesson.

....

....

....

....

In your group, discuss and plan how you could use assembly time to help others to learn and understand how to make the school a healthier place. How might you persuade them to commit themselves to healthier behaviour?

Write your ideas here.

....

....

....

....

....

....

....

....

....

....

....

(18) People needing special help
Can you help me?

Preparation/materials

activity sheets 1 (one per group) and 2 (one each). Consider children with special needs in your class, and how you might usefully incorporate these (and other real-life examples from your class) in this lesson. The lesson aims to help children explore 'asking for and offering help', and to understand and respect the particular cases of disability and special needs as just part of a wider picture.

Key words

please
disastrous
inconvenient
cerebral palsy
civil servants

Skills

deciding when to help;
understanding special needs for help

Kick start

Ask all the children in your class to think of when they last asked for help from someone.

Take some examples. Ask why they needed help (too hard, I couldn't do it; too heavy, I couldn't lift it by myself; I didn't believe I could do it, I needed encouragement; I didn't know, so I asked someone who did! I'd forgotten, I needed reminding). A show of hands for the categories that emerge can quickly include everyone. Is there anyone in the class who doesn't ever need help? Is there *anyone* who doesn't need help? Explore this a little, establishing that everyone could do with help at times (including parents, teachers, police officers, doctors and even government ministers, who rely upon civil servants).

Activity 1

What did the children say when they asked for help? Ask them to tell you how they asked. (I said, 'Please!'; I said, 'Excuse me...'; I shouted, 'Help!') How did they feel when they asked for help? What was going on inside their heads? (Good – I can get the help I need! Embarrassed – Oh no, I can't manage! Nervous – what will they think of me? Worried – what if they say 'no'? Frightened – they'll think I'm silly.) Add any new words to your class Circle of Feelings.

Does everyone who needs help always ask for it? What happens if people don't ask for help when they need it? Divide the class into groups and ask every group to make up two stories, each with a character who needs help but doesn't ask for it. Ask them to specify the name, age and situation in each story, and use them to illustrate two different outcomes from *not* asking for help. They could use activity sheet 1 for this.

Extension

Use examples from the stories to explore how important it can be to ask for help, what might happen if they don't, and the likely feelings in each case. Explore when the children think it would be disastrous not to ask (Grab my hand – I'm falling!) and when they judge it might just be an inconvenience (I could do this more quickly if you would be kind enough to help me!) and some points in between. Also, when might it be good? (I was stuck on this sum but I didn't ask for help and, look, I've managed to do it by myself!) Encourage the children to feel comfortable with asking for help whenever they need it.

Activity 2

Did anyone in their stories have any type of disability? If so, or if there is disability in the class, you might use this as a starting point. If not, ask the stories' writers why none featured disabilities. Have they fallen into a stereotype trap?

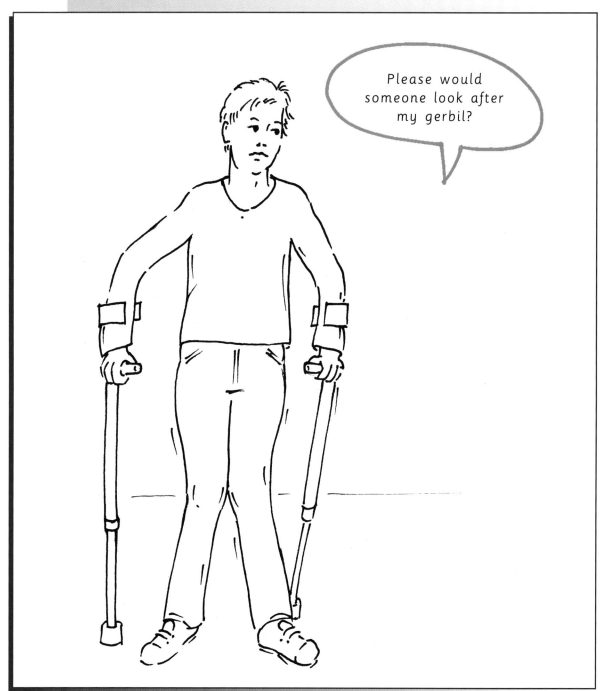

Ask what people with disabilities can do well. (Some people with learning difficulties can run really fast in races! Some blind people can hear and smell better than sighted people. Some people who need wheelchairs to get around can tell great stories! There are some really excellent, caring parents with only one arm! Having to use crutches doesn't stop you being good at sums!) Do people with disabilities ask for help? Explore this idea a little, establishing that some don't need help – they are good at what they are doing. Others are just like everyone else – they may need help with something and may ask, if they feel comfortable doing so, or they may be too nervous, or frightened. Ask everyone in the class to use activity sheet 2 to draw a picture of a situation where someone who has a disability is asking for help, and then briefly write descriptions of what happened. Encourage them to avoid falling into the trap of assuming the disability is always visible! Use examples from their stories to illustrate the range of situations where help may be requested. Did anyone's story have a person asking for help that had nothing to do with their disability? ('My character has brittle bones and she was asking for help with her homework.' 'Mine has cerebral palsy and finds it quite hard to walk. He wanted someone to look after his gerbil while he was away for the weekend!')

Extension

Help the class to explore two further dimensions – the responsibility of the person approached in deciding whether to say yes, or to refuse; and the skill in judging when it is responsible and caring to *offer* help. (When could you offer to help someone? When might your help be *refused*? Is it OK to refuse help? Does it mean you shouldn't offer it?) Ask the class to invent examples to represent possible scenarios, and not to forget that their characters might sometimes have special needs. Ask contributors to suggest the feelings of all characters in each situation, and use these to strengthen the children's understanding of helping.

Reflect and act

Everyone needs help sometimes! It's OK to ask. It's OK to offer, (and to be turned down). Before next week, see if you can ask for help when you need it, find an opportunity to offer help, and find a time when you can help someone who asks you.

Lesson 18
Activity Sheet 1 *Can I manage?*

Draw and describe two situations where someone needs help but doesn't ask for it. Say why not and what happens. Give your characters names and ages.

Situation 1

Situation 2

Name _____ **Date** _____

Lesson 18
Activity Sheet 2 — *I need help!*

Draw a situation where someone who has a disability or a special need wants help and asks for it. Describe underneath what is happening, why they need help and the outcome of the situation. Give your characters names and ages.

Here is my character asking for help:

In this box, write down everything that happens.

This is what happens:

(19) Rights, responsibilities
By rights...

Preparation/materials

activity sheets 1 and 2 (one of each for group)
The activities in this lesson pursue the meanings and significance of 'rights' (those claims to freedoms, treatment, access, etc. which are conferred by birth or by rules or laws) and 'responsibilities' (duties, obligations, and the state of being answerable). You may decide to gather some information about the UN Convention on the Rights of the Child. You can access detailed information, from the following website:
http://www.unicef.org/crc/
Activity 2 requires large sheets of paper (one per group) and colouring materials for illustrations.

Key words

right
definition
confer
Convention
fundamental
origin

Skills

to recognise the rights of oneself;
to recognise the rights of others

Kick start

Ask the class to tell you what the word 'right' means. (Correct, just, a direction, to put right, a claim, etc.)

Establish that you want to talk about the noun form of the word, meaning 'claim'. Ensure everyone understands the meaning of 'definition'. Ask for, or offer, a definition of a table, a cat, weather, etc. as clarifying examples if necessary. You could also ask the children to suggest one or two definitions, with a challenge to the rest of the class to guess what these define! Explain that you want the children to help you to define 'right', but that you are first going to help them to explore what it means and where rights come from.

Activity 1

*Can the children suggest a 'right' that they have at school? When their hand is up and the teacher chooses them, do they have a **right to** speak, or is it just **permission?** What about being treated respectfully by others in the class? This is a **right** established by the class ground rules.*

Divide the class into small groups, (four or so) and challenge them to produce a list of the rights they believe they have, and to say where each has come from, i.e. who 'says' (has established) it's a right. Activity sheet 1 provides space for their ideas, and permission to write down things they aren't sure are rights! Encourage them to reject anything for which they have, or obtain, *permission*, and things they think they *should be allowed to do* (stay up to watch a TV programme, eat chips twice a week, get Man U's latest strip, etc.) and to focus on *rights* conferred by rules, laws or agreements. Take feedback, and ask the children to underline the rights that you and the rest of the class confirm. Check they understand that (most) legislative rights come from parliament and the democratic process. They may have heard of human rights, and perhaps have listed some. Note where they think these come from, and who says so!

The rights of pupils in this class

1. Everyone has a right to respect
2. We all have a right to be allowed to learn
3. Everybody has the right to their own opinion
4. We all have a right to go out at break times
5. We have a right to bring our toys to school if we don't play with them in class.
6. We have a right to choose what we eat.
7. We have a right to stay at home when we don't feel well.
8. We have ...

Extension

Explain that there are fundamental rights to which **every** child is entitled, regardless of where born or to whom, regardless of gender, religion or social origin. Clarify the meaning of 'fundamental' if necessary, and ask for ideas as to what these rights are, inviting each group to add these rights (once agreed to be such by class consensus) to their lists.

Tell the class the United Nations generated a rights list, much as the class is doing now, by members getting together and discussing what it should contain. The list was published in 1989 as The Convention on the Rights of the Child, and has been signed by (almost) every country in the world. The Convention says all children were *born* with these rights. They include rights to survival, health and education; to a caring family environment, play and culture; to protection from exploitation and abuse of all kinds; and to have their voices heard and opinions taken into account on significant issues. There are international laws to protect these rights! If there is a school council, draw a parallel between the UN (representatives from each country) and the School Council (representatives from each class). Can the children remember the care with which they listened to each other's views and opinions in Lesson 4? (See lesson 4, activity 2 extension.) And since?

Activity 2

Give each group a large sheet of paper, and ask them to discuss, agree the design, and then produce a poster to publicise child rights. Rough ideas can be set out on activity sheet 2.

Hands reach out from the side of a truck transporting people who lived up to two years in refugee camps in Zaire, back home, on a road near the town of Ruhengeri.

By end November 1996, some 640,000 Rwandans who had lived up to two years in refugee camps in eastern Zaire had returned to Rwanda in a few weeks' time-frame. Together with other UN agencies and NGOs, UNICEF provided relief aid along the road from the border town of Gisenyi, where the vast majority re-entered the country, while supporting Government efforts directing people to continue to their home districts.

Of some 5,000 children separated from their parents during the return, most were reunited with family members either near Gisenyi or in their communes of origin. UNICEF teams also visited Zairean towns, including Goma and Sake, as well as former refugee camp areas, in search of unaccompanied Rwandan refugee children who were then transported back to Rwanda for care and family tracing.

The Convention

on the Rights of the Child

Their posters could *state* one or more rights, might show their *origin*, but must try to find a way to *illustrate* the subject and celebrate its significance. Display their posters, and then chair a discussion on their creative talents and how successfully they feel they have depicted the subject and its value. Are they pleased with their work?

Ask if they now think they are ready to define 'right'. Help them to produce a definition that uses their own words, and with which they all agree. This could be a banner heading for the poster display. Look for some volunteers from the class who could produce this banner.

Where can they find out about rights (benefit rights, consumer rights, etc.)? Challenge them to research this and bring their findings back to the class! They may discover the local Citizens' Advice Bureau, the public library, internet sites, etc.

Extension

Can the children suggest uses for their posters? Might they be displayed elsewhere in the school to raise the subject of school rules and rights (and the responsibilities that go with them) with other classes? Judge if it is a suitable moment for rights and responsibilities to be spotlighted (perhaps to reinforce, perhaps to review and extend current understanding and provision). This could be the subject for an assembly, a Citizenship Theme for the school, or be addressed by the School Council.

Could a school council be proposed if one doesn't yet exist? It could be modelled on the United Nations! This idea links with the theme of a whole-school approach to giving pupils a voice. The children in your class already have a voice and some understanding of the subject: their work might act as the springboard for action. This is one of several elements in this lesson which link to the National Healthy School Standard.

Reflect and act

Remind the children that rights are there to value and protect *everyone*. They are not there to give one person an advantage (or 'win') over another. Encourage the children to know their rights and be prepared to state them if they need to, but be ready to help protect the rights of others, too, whether at home or elsewhere.

Lesson 19

Activity Sheet 1 *It's everyone's right!*

On the left, write down examples of what your group believes are your rights. Next to each, say where your group thinks the right has come from. You can write down things you aren't sure about or don't agree on – just put a ring around these. There will be a class discussion afterwards.

We think these are some of our rights	*We think this is where the right has come from*
....	....
....	....
....	....
....	....
....	....
....	....
....	....
....	....
....	....
....	....
....	....
....	....

Names _____ **Date** _____

_____

_____

Lesson 19

Activity Sheet 2 *Our poster!*

Write down your group's rough ideas for a rights poster!

Some rights our poster could show:

To illustrate the value of our rights, our poster might look like this:

By rights...
Real Health for Real Lives © Adrian King, Noreen Wetton, Nelson Thornes Ltd 2003

20 Pets and pests
Cute or what?

Preparation/materials

activity sheets 1 and 2
Is there a class or school pet? Goldfish and stick insects count! If not, ask if a small-caged pet like a gerbil or hamster could be borrowed from someone's home, in time for the lesson. Ideally, ask if it can stay a day or two. (This lesson assumes some pupil knowledge of human rights, perhaps through having completed lesson 19.)

Key words

creature
habitat
neuter
spay
veterinary surgeon
(litter, brood, etc.)

Skills

To be able to empathise with domestic and wild creatures;
to be able to state, and meet, some of their needs;
to know the basic rights the law confers on animals

Kick start

Ask the class to remind you of some fundamental human rights. Enquire whether the children believe that animals have any fundamental rights. If there seems to be uncertainty or disagreement, give them an opportunity to discuss this question briefly in small huddles.

After a few minutes, take feedback and note (on board or chart) rights they consider animals to have and (any contentions to the contrary, perhaps in the form 'We believe animals don't have rights because…').

Activity 1

Explain that you are going to give the children an opportunity to speak for animals by pretending to be an animal. What might animals say if they could talk? Tell the class you would like them to split into five groups, each with one animal or bird to think about, taken from the following groups:

farm, (cow, pig, lamb, chicken, etc.); **zoo**, (ape, tiger, lion, elephant, etc.); **pest**, (rat, fox, pigeon, grey squirrel, etc.); **wild**, (hedgehog, rabbit, mole, Dartmoor pony, etc.); and **rare or endangered** (golden eagle, bank vole, red squirrel, etc.). If necessary, explain that pets will be considered later!

We think animals have these rights:

- a right to be cuddled!

- a right to be left alone!

- a right to a vet when they are ill!

- a right to build their nest or burrow

- a right to feed

- protection from cruelty

- a right to play

- a right to water

- a right to enough space if they are not free

We think animals do not have rights because:

- they are only animals

- they do not understand rights

- they are only there for us to eat or enjoy

- how can they have rights if they can't tell us what they are?

- I do not like animals!

My waters run dry, my waters run dry

I don't like animals

Ask the class to suggest one or more examples for each group. Use the examples from page 126 if they are short of ideas! Allot each group a category and one of its animals/birds to think about. (Can the pest group say what characteristics make something a 'pest'? They may agree this can depend who is doing the defining. Farmers call dogs pests when they attack sheep. Mice might consider cats pests!) 'Rare or endangered' may prove the hardest – though the group could be enthusiastic about a non-indigenous animal like a blue whale or a snow-leopard, these are not likely to yield changes to understanding about local (UK) responsibilities! Allow this group to substitute an animal from another category if they find this one too hard.

Ask each group to think of areas of animal life they could consider (habitat, availability of food, how people treat them, protection, cruelty) and then think what their animal might say about how it would like to be treated, if only it could talk and think as we do. Encourage each group to decide how they will present their ideas to the class in a way that includes all members of their group, and then take feedback from all the groups. (Perhaps each could state one 'wish': 'I am a rabbit and I want people who find my burrow to leave it unblocked!' 'I am a golden eagle, and please leave my eggs alone! It took a long time to build my nest and I want to see my babies hatch and fly.')

Extension

Invite the children to repeat the exercise for a pet, again giving each group a different example, preferably of their choosing (cat, dog, budgerigar, goldfish, tortoise, pony, etc.). How would they like to be treated by their owners, and what might they say? 'I am a dog and I need fresh water every day!' 'I am a budgie and I don't like it when people bang my cage!'

⒇ Pets and pests Cute or what?

Activity 2

When contributions have been made, ask if the children think any of their ideas (from any group) are common to all five categories and therefore to all animals/birds. Are they just hopes and wishes, or are they needs?

Return to fundamental human rights – ask how useful they think it would be to say that all animals have *'a right to education'*…or *'to have their voices heard'*? Explain that it is because animals cannot speak that we have to assess their needs and to speak for them, and to set out basic rights to govern the way we treat them. What about *'a right to protection from cruelty and abuse'*? Does that apply to animals as well as people? Invite the children to have a discussion (in the whole class or in groups) to identify the needs all creatures have, and whether these could be considered rights. Encourage discussion about *'a right to survival'* and how this conflicts with the way we treat pests and kill animals for food. Include children who are vegetarian in the debate if you have any, and even animals if anyone wishes to speak for them! ('I am a lamb and I think…' or 'I think a chicken might say…'). Do endangered species have a *greater* right to survival than sheep or cows? Take varying opinions! After the discussion has ranged widely, invite everyone to narrow their thinking and focus on pets, to suggest *their* rights, and to list these on activity sheet 1. A class composite could emerge…

I think a cow might say 'I'm a vegetarian - you could be one, too!'

There are laws to protect animals from cruelty, whether on farms or in homes. Do the children know the names of any organisations that help enforce these laws? Perhaps they could try to find out! (RSPCA, RSPB, SSPCA, etc. For a good UK listing go to: http://www.animalrescuers.co.uk and click *Rescuers: UK Wildlife Centres*, or *Rescuers: National/International*.

Can the children use the internet to discover more? To pursue the subject of wildlife further, you can find some downloadable teaching resources from the World Wildlife Fund UK website, at: http://www.wwflearning.co.uk/resource/

Extension

Remind the class that rights and responsibilities often go together. The class ground rules are a good example – they are there to protect everyone's rights and needs, and make the classroom a comfortable place to be and to learn, but everyone has a responsibility to try to keep them, and to encourage others to. It's different with animals and their needs and rights. They cannot take responsibility, so we have to! Invite the class to write and illustrate on activity sheet 2 some advice to pet-owners that takes account of animal rights and needs, and sets out the responsibilities we take on when we have pets. Who takes responsibility for the class/borrowed pet? Use this creature to help the children put their ideas into practice!

Reflect and act

Animals cannot speak, but considering what they might say can be a good way of helping people decide how to treat them. Remind the children that whenever they and others see animals, they have responsibilities to respect their rights and needs!

Name _____ **Date** _____

Lesson 20

Activity Sheet 1 — *All right, pet!*

In the space, write down the rights you believe pets have. Some of these may be the same as human rights. Tick the ones you think are different. If there is space, draw some animals being treated well.

> I think these are some rights all pets have

Lesson 20

Activity Sheet **2** *So you want a pet?*

Write some good advice for all pet owners. Give advice about what they should all be careful to do, and include anything they should be sure to avoid doing, too!

Advice for everyone who has a pet.	
Advice about what you should do	Avoid these things
....	....
....	....
....	....
....	....
....	....
....	....
....	....
....	....
....	....
....	....
....	....
....	....
....	....
....	....
....	....
....	....
....	....

Sensitive issues 1 – The world of drugs

(21) Attitudes to drugs

What an attitude!

Preparation/materials

activity sheets 1 and 2
You may need multiple
copies of activity sheet 2,
one for each interview the
child undertakes. The time
needed for interviews means
this lesson has a protracted
time scale. Leaflets for
lesson 22 could be usefully
ordered now! (See lesson
22, Preparation.)
* See also page 198, *Health
for Life 8–11*, Nelson
Thornes, 2000

Key words

elicit
interviewee
respondent
perspective
prejudice
objective
variation

Skills

being able to consider own
and others' attitudes;
understanding the
importance of perspective,
facts and objectivity;
grasping how prejudice can
grow from unbalanced
messages;
reviewing own attitudes

Kick start

Ask the class to tell you as many names of *non-medicinal** drugs as they can (*any drugs used for non-medical purposes). It doesn't matter if the names are incorrect, slang street names or brand names, or if you get more than one name for the same thing.

Write down the pool of ideas on the board or chart, and keep handy. The children may have done the same thing on other occasions – a similar exercise focusing on medicines is part of lesson 23 in Real Health for Real Lives, 8–9 – but in both cases it is important that the names come from them.

Activity 1

Set the class a first task to establish the two drugs that they would most like to highlight for the next three lessons. You may need to help them correct names, and ensure slang is understood before they start choosing.

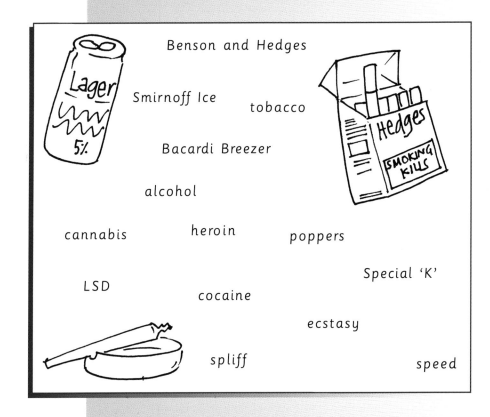

Benson and Hedges

Lager

Smirnoff Ice

tobacco

Bacardi Breezer

alcohol

cannabis   heroin   poppers

Special 'K'

LSD   cocaine

ecstasy

spliff   speed

Suggest they gather in huddles and consider which drugs they want to focus on (one they have seen on sale in the street, one that frightens them, one they know little about, one they think they know lots about but want to check, etc.). If they have trouble agreeing just two, they can choose one or two 'reserves'. Take 'bids' from each huddle, underlining the main two they pick, to build up a shortlist on the board. Next, ask for any of the 'reserves' that aren't yet highlighted. The second task, for the whole class, is to reduce the shortlist to three or four. Chair a short discussion, listening to their reasons. If time compels, choose for them, but be led by the children and reassure them their studies do not end with this selection! The children can write the names of the chosen three or four on activity sheet 1. Keep a copy of the pool of drugs and its shortlist for future reference. (If it is your intention to provide adequate lesson time during the term for the class to focus on each drug in their list, a separate class task could be to prioritise the whole shortlist.)

Extension

Next comes an attitude activity (it has no right answers and doesn't depend on knowledge). Ask the class to give some impressions of the three or four drugs on activity sheet 1. They may like a chance to reflect briefly on their views, feelings, preconceptions or experiences before setting down their own individual portrait of the drug in 'face and words'. Can they draw the drug in the form of a face, and add words of their own to describe it? Or perhaps draw their own face with an expression to match their feelings.

(21) Attitudes to drugs: What an attitude!

Activity 2

This activity needs a series of prepared questions, carefully crafted by the children to probe the attitudes of other people about these drugs. Set them a challenge to compose the best questions they can, to elicit responses which effectively reveal the attitudes of their respondents. This may be best done in groups. (Trust is not a key feature in this composing exercise, so it presents an opportunity for random or changed groupings.)

The questions we thought of are:

1 What three words do you think of when you hear the word (drug name)?

2 Which of these three (four) drugs would you like to see banished from the planet? (Give names)

3 Imagine a friend of yours becomes a regular user of (drug name). Realistically, how do you think the story is most likely to end?

4 What could be done to make things better in relation to (drug name)?

(Questions 1, 3 and 4 need to be asked for each drug in turn.)

Take some feedback, and choose up to half a dozen questions which consensus or a vote indicate could be the most effective in gauging the attitudes to the chosen drugs. A list of people to interview is now needed – to range quite widely in age and background. Ask the class for ideas – including people they would like to interview, but can't! Write them on the board.

Discuss what can be done about the 'unavailable' group. Could the children imagine what it is like to be these people: (very busy, a long way away, do not speak English, etc.) Can they imagine what these people might think about these drugs? Could someone pretend to be the Prime Minister? a grower? a dealer? If suitable players emerge, they can be interviewed! Apportion tasks, preferably from volunteers, so that everyone has one or two interviews, or is a stand-in for an absent interviewee. Decide whether everyone will ask questions about all the drugs, or whether to 'share' them. The questions and answers could be noted on activity sheet 2. They will need a separate sheet for each interview. Establish the time frame. Can they be done over the weekend? During half-term? By this time next week?

People we could interview:	People we would like to interview but can't:
priest, imam, rabbi	Prime Minister
parents and carers	a dealer, sales person
the milkman	farmer/grower
older brother/sister	police officer
auntie/uncle/nan/grandad	
head teacher	
(some!) next door neighbours	
someone our age in another class or school	

Reflect and act

Remind the children that attitudes about drugs differ. Others may have a different perspective, and experiences. Even their own attitudes can change. Suggest they ask themselves: "Am I right to feel as I do?"

Extension

Collect and discuss the results. Any surprises? All the same or huge variation? Why might there be differences of feeling or opinion? (Better/worse informed, personal experience, a financial interest, objective, prejudiced by media coverage, not very interested, frightened, etc.) How convincing were the stand-ins' answers? Which of the answers does the class agree with? How many interviewees seemed to be objective, and how many had a narrow, perhaps prejudiced, perspective? How different were the grower's/dealer's views? Give everybody a chance to say if their own attitudes have changed as a result of the interviews the class have conducted, and to explain (if they feel comfortable to do so). Taken together, can they learn anything about the drugs in question from these answers? Discuss how the results could be displayed on paper or using the computer. Keep them for reference.

Lesson 21
Activity Sheet 1 *With attitude!*

Write down the three (or four) drugs your class has chosen, one in each space. Below the name, draw a face with an expression that tells how you feel about this drug. Around the drawing, write the words that say how you feel – as many as you like. Do the same for the other drugs. There are no wrong answers...

Name of drug	Name of drug ....
Name of drug	Name of drug ....

Lesson 21
Activity Sheet 2

Questions, questions!

Write down the questions agreed by the class, and the answers you receive. Please thank your interviewee for their help.

Category of person being interviewed (parent, milkman, Rabbi, etc.)

....

Subject drug ....

Questions	Answers
1..	1..
....	....
....	....
....	....
....	....
....	....
....	....
....	....
....	....
....	....
....	....
....	....
....	....
....	....

㉒ Facts about drugs

That's a fact!

* See also page 198, *Health for Life 8–11*, Nelson Thornes, 2000

Preparation/materials

activity sheets 1 and 2 (one each for group). You will need some reliable sources of drug facts: books, leaflets, telephone helplines, websites or your own prepared handouts. A useful government leaflet is *Drugs: The Facts* available in quantity, free from 0800 555777. On the website *Wired for Health* (www.wiredforhealth.gov.uk) there are two sections which may contain some suitable content. The KS2 section is at www.galaxy-h.gov.uk. The KS3 section, at www.lifebytes.gov.uk., contains detailed information about drugs – judge its suitability carefully! For reliable information for teachers, go to www.wiredforhealth.gov.uk and click 'teachers' then 'teaching and learning'

Key words

medicinal
crucial
prohibited
hazardous
beneficial
legitimate

Skills

seeking facts;
judging the quality of sources;
questioning information;
acting on reliable information;
trusting the person but not necessarily their information

Kick start

Ask the class to tell you one thing they know about one of the class-spotlighted drugs.

Take several answers and thank the providers. Tell them you plan to help them check these 'facts' later for accuracy, but now you are more concerned about where information comes from.

Activity 1

Ask: Where did they find out what they know? (Friends, magazines, newspapers, parents, older brothers, TV.) Are they sure they remembered correctly? Are they sure the paper, TV, parent, friend was right? What if they weren't right? What could go wrong if someone believed incorrect information? Pursue this, to establish that accurate information is crucial, and that knowing that facts are reliable is the key. Ask for ideas about how they can find out if their 'facts' are correct – (check; go to a reliable source).

Ask how the children can be sure that a source is reliable. (I trust him; papers and TV are always right; *their* sources got it right; compare sources, etc.) If they don't suggest comparing sources, suggest it yourself, and ask for ideas about how the class could try this. One way is for groups to use activity sheet 1 to pool some facts about the class-spotlighted drugs they think are right and then check them against a source you can vouch for (leaflet, website, prepared handout). Judge whether each group needs to concentrate on one drug, or all of them. The activity sheet is set up for one. When they have finished, ask for feedback. Have all their facts been checked? Were any corrections needed after checking? What have they discovered that is new? Was there anything (local information, prices, related experience, slang names, etc.) that they couldn't check? Who/where could they ask about these things? How sure could they be about the answers they get? (Ask at least three people, ask police or local drugs agency, compare notes, etc.)

Extension

The class is now in a position to pool all the checked facts, and anything new they have discovered, and produce a compilation for each of the drugs in focus. Decide if this is useful! If so, they should bear in mind the reasons why they focused on their chosen drugs, and try to ensure all their queries and anxieties are addressed. They may now be ready to embark upon a similar exercise with the next drug on the highlighted list from lesson 22.

(22) **Facts about drugs:** That's a fact!

Activity 2

Are their chosen drugs legal or illegal? If they are legal, does your school ever authorise their possession, sale or use on the premises? (Wine provided at governors' meetings, etc.) You may need to familiarise yourself with any stipulations your school drugs policy makes about legal drugs at school.

Ask the class to look back at the highlighted list of drugs from lesson 21. Can they say which are legal and which are illegal? Can they ever be both? (Some drugs can be illegal without a prescription e.g. heroin; alcohol is legal for over 18s to buy but not for younger people; cigarettes are legal for children to possess, but not to sell, etc.) Do the school rules forbid some drugs, even when they are legal to possess? What else does the school drugs policy say about which drugs are prohibited or legitimate? Remind the class that all the drugs they highlighted were drugs used for non-medical purposes. Ask them to research what rules and laws say about these drugs. Make sure they use a reliable source! They can use activity sheet 2, and write on the back if necessary. Each group will need to choose someone to write the group's discoveries on the activity sheet. Could this be the beginnings of a class drugs encyclopaedia?

Extension

Congratulate the class on having checked facts, and becoming well-informed. Tell them this is a very responsible thing to do, and is just as important in other areas of life. Ask them to think of some other examples where it is crucial that they know their information and its sources are reliable (buying second-hand items, using public transport, finding out about consumer rights, knowing the times of tides, etc.). Can they give examples of where wrong information led (or might lead) to unwanted outcomes such as annoyance, frustration, waste of time or money, or even disaster?

Reflect and act

After this lesson, ask the children whether their attitudes to these drugs have changed at all. If so, what changed them (facts, others' views, etc.)? Remind them that seeking facts, and reflecting on their own attitudes, and questioning them are very responsible ways to behave. It helps them become sources of views and information others can rely on!

Lesson 22
Activity Sheet 1) *Oh, really?*

1 Discuss and write down the things your group believes they know about this drug.

We think these facts are true:

2 Tick the facts you confirm as true and put a question mark if you can't find out. If there is space, write any corrections.

This is what we found out when we checked:

✓ ?

3 In this space, write down anything new you discovered about the drug.

Names _____ **Date** _____

_____

_____

Lesson 22

Activity Sheet 2 *It's the law!*

Write the names of the drugs your class highlighted in this column.

Name of drug:

In this column, write down what the law says and what your school rules say about each drug.

This is what we found out:

....

....

....

....

....

....

....

....

....

....

....

....

....

....

....

(turn over if you need more space)

That's a fact!
Real Health for Real Lives © Adrian King, Noreen Wetton, Nelson Thornes Ltd 2003

23 Media treatment of drugs
Shock! Horror!

Preparation/materials

activity sheet 1 – one per group, and activity sheet 2. Collect some press cuttings relating to drugs. Try to include at least one featuring each of: a medicine (new one being developed, saved a life, shortage in less-developed country, etc.); a legal-but-non-medicinal drug (such as alcohol, tobacco, poppers, etc.); and one depicting illegal drugs, their suppliers, their users, or the consequences of illegal use. You will need enough copies for every small group to see at least one.

Key words

imply
exaggeration
emotive
balanced
neutral
manipulate

Skills

recognising manipulative writing;
learning not to trust the media blindly;
knowing what skills may help in situations involving drugs;
recognising and assessing their own need to develop further skills

Kick start

Ask the children to suggest some (fictitious) newspaper headlines. (Summer here at last! Dog bites postman! France sinks without trace! School finds oil under playground!)

Now request some more, this time about drugs. (Drugs found in library! Prime Minister jailed for having Crack! Head Teacher smokes spliff in staffroom!) Congratulate all the class journalists.

Activity 1

Though there may be humour or disaster in their efforts, point out the predominance, if the case, of a negative image of drugs in their headlines heralding reports of situations we would not want to occur, and perhaps illegal ones as well.

Did their headlines all imply that illegal drugs were featured in the subsequent reports? Were any about medicines? If not, ask why this was? (Headlines are often about shock, and bad news; good news is not so eye-catching, etc.) Tell the class that the skills they have been learning about drugs are now going to be put to good use, to judge the efforts of real journalists.

Divide the class into groups of three or four and give each a copy of one of the news clippings. There is probably some information reported in each that it is not possible for the children to check. Their main task, however, is to assess the quality of the clipping. Can they find out from the clipping the attitude of the writer to the featured drug and those involved with it? Or was the writer neutral? Which words tell them this? Which adjectives contribute most to the picture painted by the item? Are they just descriptive or are they emotive? Do they appear especially negative? Positive? Is there anything the writer wants the reader to think, but isn't actually written? (This is called *implying*.) Which words do this job? There is space for much of this task on activity sheet 1.

CHILDREN'S HARD WORK AMAZES TEACHER!

Children at a local school shocked and surprised their teacher yesterday. One class worked so hard they didn't want to stop at the end of the day. They were all still working quietly in small groups at breakfast time next morning. "We worked all night!" they told our reporter.

Extension

Are any 'facts' about the drug included? If yes, are they correct? Exaggerated? If not entirely accurate, why might that be? The children may suggest that some news writers want to produce emotions and sell newspapers more than educate their readers! How balanced is the item – does it report everyone's viewpoint, or just the writer's? Discuss any differences between reporting of illegal drugs, legal drugs and medicines. How *neutral* does their writer seem to be? And how *accurate*? Overall, how many marks out of 10 would each group give their journalist? Compare the marks! What have the children learned from this analysis?

Activity 2

You may want to check that everyone understands and supports the ground-rules before the next activity particularly any dealing with respect and keeping confidences.

keeping safe and healthy;   being careful;
asking for advice or help;   making good decisions;
telling the teacher;   knowing when to see the doctor;
finding out facts;   following instructions;
checking information is right;   searching the internet;
sticking to a decision;   keeping calm in an emergency.

Ask the children to put their hands up. Ask them to keep them up until you mention a drug they think may have been used or tried by someone they know. If you judge it to be appropriate, mention cannabis, to establish that illegal drugs are included in your thinking. You may omit it, if not. Then go through a list like: tobacco, alcohol, insulin, Ventolin (or other asthma inhaler), Paracetamol, Calpol, and lastly caffeine (found in tea, coffee, etc.). Any hands still up? Is it fair to call ours a drug-using society? Now pose the question to the class to ponder on: what skills are needed by someone growing up and living in a drug-using society? Invite them to talk about this and to consider matters like safety, judgement, knowledge, understanding, help. Take feedback and pool the answers. Can the class help you highlight the half-dozen (choose an appropriate number) most important skills?

Extension

Which of these skills are only useful in relation to drugs? (There may be none!) Which of these skills are represented in the class? Not everyone will feel they have all those represented. Can they say which skills they are good at, which they need more practice at, and which they still need to develop? Action sheet 2 is for writing this down. If a ready list of skills emerges from this exercise that the class agrees they need to practise or develop, they may need your help!

Reflect and act

Remind the children that accurate knowledge is important. Their health is even more important! They can use their knowledge to safeguard their health and keep themselves safe – as long as they develop and use the right skills.

(Lesson 23)
Activity Sheet) I) *News!*

The headline from our news clipping is:

....

Read your news clipping out to the group. Are there some words that tell you the writer's attitude to the drug in the clipping?

These words tell us the writer's attitude:

....

....

What kind of 'picture' is painted by the report?

....

....

These adjectives contribute most strongly to the picture:

....

....

What does the writer want you to think about the drug in the report?

....

....

Is this written clearly, or just implied?

Agree in your group to give the writer marks out of 10:

for being neutral [ ]   for accuracy [ ]   overall [ ]
                         (about the drug)

Name _____   **Date** _____

Lesson 23
Activity Sheet 2 *Skilled!*

Write down the skills your class decided are important for children growing up in a drug-using society. Put a different number next to each. Draw a ring round the ones some children in your class feel they have.

....

....

....

Here is a space to write down your skills (just write the numbers).

I am good at these skills: ....

....

I want to practise these skills: ....

....

I need to develop these skills: ....

....

Draw a picture with yourself in it, using one of the skills.

The skill I am using is: ....

Sensitive issues 2 – keeping myself safe

(24) Resisting the persuaders

I can make choices!

Preparation/materials

activity sheets 1 and 2 – one per group
* See also page 226, *Health for Life 8–11*, Nelson Thornes, 2000

Key words

negative influence
exert
bribery
blackmail
deceptive
apparent
verbal

Skills

understanding influences, being able to resist pressure or persuasion; recognising positive influences

Kick start

How many of the class watched TV yesterday evening? What did they watch? Were the programmes good? Was it BBC, ITV, Sky? Cable? Digital?

Did the programmes have breaks for advertising? What were the advertisements advertising? Write a list as they tell you. Who doesn't remember the adverts? Who doesn't watch them? What do they do instead? Who didn't watch TV at all yesterday? What did *they* do? (Read a book, played with my brother, helped put my little sister to bed, rode my bike in the garden, took the dog for a walk.)

Activity 1

Ask the children to imagine they want someone to do something for them. What might it be? What could they say? Supposing the person refused – what else could they say? Can they think of a strategy to persuade them? (Promise something in return, bribery, threats, blackmail, make it sound really attractive.)

Supposing they wanted the person to buy something from them – how could they make it seem desirable? (Clean it up, offer it at a cut price, say 'you can't get them any more!') What if it was brand new – how could they persuade people to buy it? (Put pretty packaging round it; make it look bigger!; offer buy-one-get-one-free; make it seem 'expensive'.) Ask the class if they ever take any notice of adverts by buying (or wanting) the items. How many admit to being influenced? How many think their parents or carers are influenced by advertising? ...or their friends? (If few do, ask why advertisers advertise if people aren't persuaded by them.)

Divide the class into groups of four or five and ask each group to write an advertisement for an item without saying exactly what it is. Decide whether to allocate item to group, or allow choice!

- a book – without saying its title or what it's about

- a film or video to watch – but without describing title or content

- an item of food – without saying what, exactly

- a toy or game – but not precisely how to play with it or what it does

- a holiday – but not where or for how long

- a gadget – but without clarity as to its function.

They may use activity sheet 1 to record their ideas.

Ask for a volunteer from each group to read theirs out and then vote for the most persuasive. Which words, ideas or images seemed to be the most effective?

Extension

Return to the list of TV adverts. Can anyone describe an advert – what it was selling, what took place, what was said? One of the characteristics of a successful advert is that it is memorable! Would they buy the item from the remembered advert?

Ask the children to tell you examples of cheaper 'own-brand' items (Tesco cornflakes, Sainsbury's baked beans, Pricerite shampoo, etc.) Are the 'top brand' versions better? Take a range of opinions! Remind them that one reason own-brand items are cheaper is because they don't advertise (so much). Tell them a short advert on the TV may cost the advertiser £50,000 or more, and that they have to pay the advertising agency, too! Who do the children think pays for advertising? Remind them that people who make the goods believe it works, or they wouldn't pay to do it. What messages do the children have for advertisers?

(24) Resisting the persuaders: I can make choices!

Ask who had the greatest influence on the children in your class when they were babies? What about when they were in infant classes? And now – who currently influences the children on the way they think and behave? (Parents, teachers, friends, advertisers, footballers, pop stars, etc.)

Did anyone say 'myself'? How big is their own influence on what they think, feel or say? Who else has a *really* big influence? Divide them into groups and ask them to focus on their *friendship groups* and to discuss what kind of influences their friends have on how they think, and what they feel, say and do. Activity sheet 2 is to pool their ideas. Discuss their findings! Do they ever feel strongly influenced – pressured – by their groups of friends? (No one does *that* any more! Those trainers are rubbish! That would be dangerous!) Can they truly make their own decisions?

Ask if they can give examples of where the influence on them has been good, and not so good. What makes an influence a good influence? (One that agrees with me! One that challenges my views and plans! One that helps me decide!) What about examples of where they have 'ignored' the influences, suggestions or pressures and decided (perhaps differently) for themselves? Have they any advice for those who *feel* trapped or pushed into doing or saying something they don't want to by those in their friendship group? Have they any advice for those (perhaps without realising it) doing the pushing or pressuring? Emphasise that sometimes, even when someone feels pressured, it may be that nobody is exerting it purposely.

Extension

If the class seems to find this exploration useful, ask them to draw a picture of a group and some pressure (real or felt but **not** a 'dare'). Say: 'Put yourself into the picture, making sure the pressure is not trapping or pushing you, or anyone else. What is being said? What are you thinking? What are *you* saying? (firmly but politely).'
Don't forget to ask the children what they have got out of this discussion. How do they feel now?

Reflect and act

Remind the children that influences are unavoidable, and may be helpful or unhelpful. But they need to stay in charge of how they behave, and do what they believe to be right and sensible. If they trust themselves, they can withstand unhelpful pressure! Can they report examples back to the class when next they happen?

Irresistible!

Write a verbal advertisement for your item. Try to describe its excellent qualities, desirable characteristics, its good value, and what is enjoyable about it. Make it sound like the best thing since sliced bread! Can you give it an *irresistible* image? Can you make the user, owner, wearer really *someone*?

Our advertisement says:

....

....

....

....

....

....

....

Can you draw the image you would like your advertisement to paint in the reader's or listener's mind?

Names _____   **Date** _____

_____

_____

Lesson 24
Activity Sheet 2) *My group!*

In your group, discuss the influences your friends have on you. Some may be unspoken! You may not all be influenced the same way! (Do you like the same pop groups? Food? Wear the same kind of clothes? What if you didn't? Do you feel the same about bullying? Drugs? Homework? School rules? How do you know – do you talk about these things?)

We think our friends influence us in these ways:

...on what we think ....

....

....

...on what we feel ....

....

....

...on what we say ....

....

....

...on what we do ....

....

....

(turn over if you need more space)

I can make choices!
Real Health for Real Lives © Adrian King, Noreen Wetton, Nelson Thornes Ltd 2003

(25) Reviewing safety skills

I can be safe!

Preparation/materials

activity sheets 1 (12) and 2 (one each)
Make a short list of circumstances where safety is dependent on following simple and well-known safety rules or instructions (high cliffs – don't climb, keep well away from the edge; stranger in a car – never get into a car alone with a stranger or someone you don't trust; red flag flying on the beach – don't swim here; crossing the road – use the Green Cross Code, use pedestrian crossings, follow lollipop person's instructions; broken glass – don't pick up with bare hands; ice – sprinkle salt; if you find used syringes and needles – don't touch, tell a teacher; etc.). You may want to substitute your own and include some that necessitate following school rules.
* See also page 226, *Health for Life 8–11*, Nelson Thornes, 2000

Key words

hazard
peril
elude
unique
irreplaceable

Skills

judging what to do to stay safe in a range of circumstances;
being ready to learn from others

Kick start

Tell the class you are going to help them see how competent they are at looking after their own safety.

Explain that you are going to give them a situation and you want them to put their hands up to tell you how to stay safe in those circumstances. Ask them to keep their hands up if they have a different idea from the person you first choose to answer. Take answers in quick-fire succession, acknowledging understanding and thanking the providers.

Activity 1

Tell the children you are going to play a team game that will commemorate their knowledge, and invite them to add to it! Their task is to challenge each other to respond with safety advice to situations they have thought of. Ask the children to think of other circumstances where they might not feel safe, or where lack of understanding or awareness might mean they were in danger.

The game is not to 'trick' or 'beat' the other teams – the winners will be the team that is voted to have helped other class members to think or learn most. Divide the class into exactly eight groups (of three or four). Ask them to record their ideas carefully, together with the safety information they consider most appropriate. They can, of course, ask you if they need any help. Give them a few minutes to compile their thoughts on activity sheet 1 (cycling, being out late, travelling on public transport, playing sports, in the countryside, in traffic, being bullied, medicines, non-medicinal drugs, strange surroundings, etc.).

Ask each group to join another group, so that the class becomes divided into four teams. Ask each team to combine the ideas from their two groups into one big list. Give each team an extra copy of activity sheet 1 for this. Suggest they spend some time as a team making sure they have selected situations they are happy with and safety information they think will be useful. Ask them to try to use contributions from every one of their members.

Ask them to decide how any new, unusual or interesting ideas are to be recorded, to act as reminders when it comes to voting, and to ensure everyone learns from them. Ask each team to decide how every team member can be involved in stating the situations and challenging the other teams to provide ideas for promoting safety.

Extension

Can the children recall what they learned about responsibilities from lesson 4? and from lesson 9 about 'critical moments'? Ask them to think how could they use this learning to add to their lists.

(25) Reviewing safety skills: I can be safe!

Activity 2

The game! Give each team in turn a chance to outline one situation, challenging the other three teams (who can confer) to provide information about how to stay safe in those circumstances.

Take each team's ideas. Refer back to the questioning team, to see what safety advice was in *their* minds. Use the agreed strategy for recording, to ensure that useful or new information is emphasised and stored. Make sure the team (or teams!) that brought it to attention are credited. Continue with the challenges, each team providing one before moving to the next team, rotating until all situations are put. By agreement, similar ones may be dropped, as long as no safety information is lost. Finally, take a vote as to which team's situations and information have led to the most learning. Congratulate your safety-conscious class on their work!

Extension

How much has everyone learned? Activity sheet 2 provides a space to record this individually, and to illustrate one situation that seemed significant from among those the class explored.

Remind the children that safety isn't only knowing what to do, it's also believing they are worth it! Every member of the class is unique, irreplaceable and valuable, and well-worth looking after!

Names _____/_____   **Date** _____

_____/_____

_____/_____

_____/_____

(Lesson 25)

Activity Sheet (1)   *Safer still!*

Try to think of situations where you might **be** in danger or **feel** unsafe.
Next to each, write down what you could do to **stay safe**.

What might I need to keep safe from?	What can I do to stay safe?
....	....
....	....
....	....
....	....
....	....
....	....
....	....
....	....
....	....
....	....
....	....
....	....
....	....
....	....

(turn over if you need more space)

I can be safe!
Real Health for Real Lives © Adrian King, Noreen Wetton, Nelson Thornes Ltd 2003

Lesson 25

Activity Sheet 2   *Yes, I know!*

On this page, make a written record of the things you learned from the team game about safety. There is space to illustrate a situation that caught your attention. Are you in the picture?

I learned: ....

....

....

....

....

....

....

....

....

....

The picture shows ....

....

㉖ When things go wrong

Oh, no!

Preparation/materials

activity sheets 1 and 2
Note: be sensitive to the
possibility that this lesson
could highlight issues such
as bereavement, bullying
and abuse, though it was
not written with this express
intent in mind.
* See also page 226, *Health
for Life 8–11*, Nelson
Thornes, 2000

Key words

deviation
hindsight
prophecy
mishap

Skills

managing mishaps;
managing self when things
go wrong;
summoning emergency
services

Kick start

Ask the class to give you some examples of a time when things didn't happen as planned or expected.

Did it matter? Was it a surprise? If so, was it a pleasant or an unpleasant one? Take some examples, noting the surprises and any 'disasters'.

Activity 1

Ask the children to consider why these deviations occur – what causes them? (Unforeseen circumstances, accident, bad planning, I was silly, incorrect information received, luck, didn't notice the critical moment, someone else's fault, etc.) How many of the children's examples were avoidable? (Could have been avoided by action they, or someone, could reasonably have been expected to take?)

What will emerge is that some unwanted outcomes can be avoided with care, thought and knowledge (if only I'd thought…); some need the benefit of hindsight or prophecy (if only I'd known…); and some were unavoidable (the tree blew down and blocked the road – nobody can change the weather! we were burgled!). Ask what can be done *after* something has 'gone wrong' (call for help, allocate blame, have a row, make the best of it, pick up 'the pieces', learn from the mistake, try to ensure it doesn't happen again).

This activity is not to consider what went wrong, or why, but to explore what happened *afterwards*. Let the children choose whether they want to work alone, in pairs, or in groups. The task is to think back to a situation where something did not go 'according to plan' and to relate what happened afterwards. Can they recall who did what? Did it make things better? Worse? What might have been done differently? Tell the children this activity is to generate discussion about how people can face and cope with a mishap, crisis or disaster, not what causes it. They may choose to present something that was well handled, or badly handled – both will provide discussion points. Activity sheet 1 provides space for their jottings.

Sensitive issues 2: Keeping myself safe

Extension

Ask the children to imagine that they see a dangerous situation arising for someone else – walking close to a cliff edge, taunting a stray dog, walking towards a patch of 'black' ice or in front of a swing, bullying. What could they do to warn or to reduce the hazard for this person? What would they say or shout? What messages do they have for people who may not be so safety conscious?

㉖ **When things go wrong:** Oh, no!

Activity 2

Take examples of both well handled and badly handled situations, from the individuals or groups who completed activity 1. Explore what was good about the way the situation was handled (how did it help? how did it make the people feel? how did it stop or minimise the damage or inconvenience? how did things improve as a result?) or what was not good (in what way was it unhelpful? what difficulties did it cause? what did it not achieve that it should have done? how did it make the people feel? what might have been handled better or more effectively?).

Discuss the pros and the cons in order to clarify what may be helpful to do (or think) and what is less so. Make sure they explore the differences between serious mishap, (fire, crime, injury, serious loss, bullying, etc.) and less serious, though inconvenient and possibly expensive events (broken Walkman, torn clothes, lost pen, forgotten appointment), but understand that both need to be responsibly managed. Ensure emergency strategies are well understood (shouting for help, phoning fire brigade, police or ambulance, administering first aid or calling for it, telling teacher/adult, etc.).

Extension

Suggest the children think about what has been learned in their class over the last two lessons, what has been reinforced for them that they already knew (dialling 999, never touch a used needle, etc.) and how to handle a mishap or unexpected event to best effect. Can they suggest ways in which their knowledge can be presented so that others in the school (adults and children) can benefit from it? They might plan an assembly, a wall chart, an illustrated storyboard, a series of posters, or they may have much better ideas! Explore the possibilities. The children could make notes on activity sheet 2.
Can you help make it happen?

Reflect and act

Remind the children that being ready to take action to stay safe, to warn or help others, and to manage crises and mishaps, is both responsible and grown-up. Tell them that this class is showing itself to be a mature group of young people.

Name _____   **Date** _____

Lesson 26
Activity Sheet (I) *Safer still!*

Draw and write about a situation where something went wrong. What happened afterwards? Who did what? How did it work out?

Briefly, this is what went 'wrong' ....
....
....
....

Afterwards, this is what happened ....
....
....
....
....

This is how it looked

(turn over if you need more space)

Oh, no!
Real Health for Real Lives © Adrian King, Noreen Wetton, Nelson Thornes Ltd 2003

Lesson 26

Activity Sheet **2** *Listen to us!*

How can you tell others what to do to stay safe, or cope in a crisis?
Think about how the teachers and the other children in your school
could learn from you. How could your class present its knowledge?

These are my (our) ideas:

....

....

....

....

....

....

....

....

....

....

....

....

....

....

....

(turn over if you need more space)

Oh, no!
Real Health for Real Lives © Adrian King, Noreen Wetton, Nelson Thornes Ltd 2003

Sensitive issues 3 – Me and my relationships

㉗ Debating anger

Debate!

Preparation/materials

activity sheets 1 and 2
Think about how you might
arrange the classroom for
the debate. A 'stage'? A big
circle?
* See also page 261, *Health
for Life 8–11*, Nelson
Thornes, 2000

Key words

debate
rage
constructive

Skills

note writing;
debating

Kick start

Invite the class to remind you what a mime is. (Action without word or sound, to show an idea, emotion, story, situation, etc.) Ask for volunteers to come out to the front of the class and mime an emotion for you.

Choose, in turn, one or more volunteers to act surprise, joy, sadness, anger. Announce the emotion openly, so that the class knows what they are looking at, and ask them to show their appreciation of the performances. Thank the volunteers.

Activity 1

Ask: What were the characteristics of the 'anger' mimes? (facial expression, jutting jaw, clenched fists.) Was there anything even more aggressive? (e.g. flailing arms, escapes of vocal expression.)

Ask how strong an emotion anger is. Answers will probably reflect its strength, but notice anyone not answering. Ask if there is anyone who doesn't agree, or who hasn't felt very strong anger. Pose the question: 'Is it OK to get angry?' but ask the class not to answer yet.

Ask them, instead to think about their answers, and to attend to two separate tasks. The first is to put themselves in the position of someone who feels it *is* OK to get angry. The task is to write notes about what such a person would say to persuade others that getting angry is acceptable. The second task is to pretend they are someone who believes it is *not* acceptable to get angry. What might *they* think and say to convince others that getting angry is not legitimate? Notes are needed for this person's ideas, too. Activity sheet 1 provides a note pad.

Remind your class that 'writing notes' means putting words and ideas on paper, with no need to write proper sentences. An author starting to think of ideas for a new story she is planning to write, might jot down notes like these:
3 characters. Country house. One finds old well in garden. Too close – falls in – hurts leg – shouts for help. Notices statue at bottom. Sun at just right angle. Statue glints. Gold?

Extension

If this seems to help preparation for the debate, invite individuals to tell the class the sort of things that make them angry, and what they do with their anger. Do they bottle it up? Do they express it? How? What if it is a close friend or a relation who has caused their anger? What effect does this have on the situation they are angry about? Does it change what they say or do? And what effect does it have on themselves – how do they feel *after* expressing their feelings?

27 Debating anger: Debate!

Activity 2

Explain that you want the class to use their notes to have a debate. Explain (or remind them!) that this means speakers putting one view or the opposite view and everyone deciding at the end which view has been most convincing.

Invite everyone to try not to make up their mind how they feel until the debate has taken place. This debate has special rules:

1 The teacher is in charge ('in the chair') and decides who can speak – and everyone must keep to the class ground rules and listen carefully. You could choose a pupil to take this role if you had a suitable one.

2 Anyone can speak, using ideas from the left side or the right side of their activity sheets.

3 They must only speak for one 'side' at a time.

4 They do not need to agree with the view they express!

5 They must start by saying 'This person believes that getting angry is OK because...' or 'This person believes that getting angry is NOT OK because...'.

6 Nobody is allowed to say they agree or disagree with a speaker – they can only say things that come from the ideas in their notes.

7 Speakers must try to make different points from the ones they have already heard, even if they thought of them, too!

8 If a speaker is called on twice by the teacher, they can speak for the opposite view if they wish, as long as they start correctly.

9 When all the views have been expressed, everyone (speakers and listeners) is invited to vote on whether getting angry is OK or not. Choose your speakers carefully – here is a chance to bolster confidence. *After the vote*, discussion is allowed. This discussion may change views again – judge whether to take a second vote later on. If your input is needed, try to legitimise anger (if people feel it), but only responsible expression of it.

Ian got angry because his mate called him 'Ginger'.

Reflect and act

Encourage the children to express anger clearly, gently and honestly – at once if possible. Tell them it is OK to feel any emotion they feel! They cannot avoid feeling how they feel, even if they wanted to! How they *express* emotions, or what they do as a result of feeling that way may be OK, but may make things worse. Remind them never to use their anger to hurt or damage and that managing feelings responsibly and sensitively is a really important part of friendships.

Extension

You might choose to tell the class the story of Vahid and Jasmine. Vahid has some irritating habits, but has no idea he is upsetting Jasmine because she says nothing, bottling up the feeling time after time, until there is no more space. The next time Vahid does something annoying or thoughtless, Jasmine says 'That does it...!' and lets out weeks or months of stored up anger in one go, to Vahid's amazement. If Jasmine had said clearly and gently what it was about Vahid that made her feel angry *the first time it happened*, Vahid may never have done it again, and their friendship mightn't have ended in a blazing row. Tell the class a good way of expressing anger when another *person* is the cause, is to say: 'When you .... I feel angry with you because .... '. Perhaps the children could fill in the blanks, using one or more fictitious situations, for practice, on activity sheet 2. (Are there any real needs such as these in the class? Use your judgement about whether to encourage use of this formula, perhaps in private, to sort out a real situation.)

Name _____ **Date** _____

PHOTOCOPIABLE

Lesson 27
Activity Sheet 1 *Rage!*

On the left, write some notes of your ideas! The notes are about what you could say to persuade others that **it is OK** to get angry. On the right, do the same thing, but this time your notes are intended to convince others that getting angry is **unacceptable**.

Notes on why it is OK to get angry | Notes on why is is not OK to get angry

.... | ....

.... | ....

.... | ....

.... | ....

.... | ....

.... | ....

.... | ....

.... | ....

.... | ....

.... | ....

.... | ....

.... | ....

.... | ....

.... | ....

.... | ....

.... | ....

Debating anger
Real Health for Real Lives © Adrian King, Noreen Wetton, Nelson Thornes Ltd 2003

Name _____ **Date** _____

Lesson 27

Activity Sheet 2 *Angry with you!*

Here are two chances to help someone express their anger constructively. Draw two people, one angry with the other, the angry person on the right. Write what caused the anger. In the speech bubble, write what the angry person says. Make it constructive!

When you..

....

I feel angry with you because...............

....

....

....

The person got angry because ....

....

When you..

....

I feel angry with you because...............

....

....

The person got angry because ....

....

Debating anger
Real Health for Real Lives © Adrian King, Noreen Wetton, Nelson Thornes Ltd 2003

(28) My behaviour affects others
What did I do...?

Preparation/materials

activity sheets 1 and 2
* See also page 261, Health for Life 8–11, Nelson Thornes, 2000

Key words

admiration
direct and indirect influence
interact
memorable

Skills

recognising behaviour may influence others;
reflecting on what makes personal interaction memorable and influential;
taking responsibility for being potentially influential;
reflecting on past influences

Kick start

Ask the children to tell you some names of people they admire (football players, pop stars, film and TV actors, friends, relations, etc.).

Take a range of examples. Ask what it is that they admire about the people they name. Some may find it harder than others to be specific about admirable qualities or attributes (I just like him! He's good at snooker! She's pretty! He's cool!).

Activity 1

Now ask for examples of people they would like to be like when they are grown up. In what way would they want to be like this person? Are they the same people as they named in the Kick start? If they are different, why is this?

Press them again about what, exactly, they want to copy, develop or become about this person. Can they identify specific aspects of personality, character, behaviour, attitude, skill, thought, appearance, etc., which attract or inspire them? Invite them to think of people they know (and who know them) who fit their 'I want to be like (*name*)' criterion. Are they older? Do any of them go to the local secondary or upper school(s)?

Can they remember when they first came to this school? Who were the 'big' boys and girls then? Who set the standard for behaving responsibly, carrying messages, helping teachers, meeting visitors, answering the phone (choose responsibilities Year 6 children in your school have!). Who in the school did they 'look up to'? copy? want to be like? Perhaps when your class were new pupils, Year 6 were not very good role models. If not, this year's Year 6 can do better! *Much* better. Perhaps they were excellent role models – in which case your class may want to be like them. Establish that younger children watch the 'big' children to see what they do, how they behave, how they deal with situations. Your class should know that, whether they want to be or not, they are in the spotlight. They are (part of) the most influential year group in their school. (Adapt what you say to suit a middle school).

Extension

Reinforce that though they may not choose to be role models, they are! For example, by behaving responsibly, they encourage younger children to be responsible, too. If they are not responsible, and they are seen, or if younger children hear about it, it could tempt them to think it is OK to be irresponsible, or rude, or cruel This influence is *indirect*. They may not actually speak to, or interact with the person they are influencing. Can they think of actual examples of their own behaviour that may have been an indirect influence on younger children (or even others their own age)? Activity sheet 1 invites them to recall the positive and negative influences that come to mind!

(28) My behaviour affects others: What did I do...?!

What about direct influences? Ask the children for examples (positive and negative) of ways we interact with people (talk to them, listen to them, smile at them, have snowball fights with them, help them, ask for help from them, push in front of them in a queue, thank them for stopping the traffic with their lollipop!).

Split the class into pairs and ask them to consider what *sort* of interactions others are likely to remember best. Stress you aren't asking them to remember examples of what they have actually done, just ideas of what might be memorable in daily life. Their answers need to fit a sentence like 'People are more likely to remember me when I .... '. Ask for some feedback, trying to identify categories of influential behaviour such as very kind, rude or hurtful, compliments, unusual behaviour, etc. Would it be the same if it looked as though it was just to get attention, or didn't seem genuine? It might be very memorable, but for not such good reasons! Ask the pairs to remember one interaction they have each had, which they think *might* be memorable, for whatever reason. Take examples and use them to establish a picture of this influential class. Encourage the children to recount instances where they may feel guilty or embarrassed that their behaviour was not good. Stress you won't be offering criticism on this occasion – you just want to establish what may be influential. You might offer your own observations of negative behaviour, anonymously, to make the point. Then ask the pairs to plan one way in which, directly or indirectly, they believe they would be setting a good example for younger children to follow. Can they make this behaviour a target?

Extension

Ask the class to try to remember some influential interactions with other people, in which they have learned something positive from the other person. Can they draw one of these, and describe it underneath? Activity sheet 2 could record these drawings. Can they remember when it happened?

Reflect and act

Encourage the children to keep in mind that when they queue patiently, or hold the door open for someone, or show appreciation for a kindness, that there may be others who will learn about their behaviour. How positive an influence can they be?

PHOTOCOPIABLE

Lesson 28

Activity Sheet 1 *Indirect influence!*

Write down some of the things you have said or done, which you think **indirectly** had a positive influence on younger children. (Only choose times when you didn't speak to or interact with them.) There is space for you to remember some of the things that may not have had such a positive influence, too! You might draw one from either list.

These things may have had a good influence on younger children	These things may have had a not-so-good influence on younger children
....	
....	....
....	....
....	....
....	....
....	....
....	....
....	....
....	....

This is me having an indirect influence!

Names _____ **Date** _____

Lesson 28

Activity Sheet 2 *I remember!*

Draw a memorable interaction between you and someone else. Choose something that you feel had a good and lasting influence on you. Briefly describe it, too. If you can remember **when** it happened, write it here:

It happened ....

```



This is what happened ..............................................................................

...........................................................................................................

...........................................................................................................

...........................................................................................................
```

(29) The sort of person I am
What am I like?

Preparation/materials

activity sheets 1 and 2.
Look back at the content
(and any available material
generated) from lessons 7,
8, 10, 11, 12, 13. This may
be useful to bear in mind
when asking the children to
recall what they have
learned about relationships
and the progress they have
made during their junior
school years. This lesson is
intended to be more about
recognition of strengths
than identifying learning
needs.
* See also page 261, *Health
for Life 8–11*, Nelson
Thornes, 2000

Key words

insight
checklist
thumbnail sketch
social skills

Skills

recognising personal
development;
valuing social skills;
comparing self image with
others' views of me;
considering gender
differences;
data collection and
presentation

Kick start

Start by asking 'What are you like, (say their name)?' and indicating to that child to answer. They may be unsure, but may say 'I'm a boy/girl'. Move on to another child with the same question. Allow several bland expressions (gender, nice, good), but after a few, say 'I know you're a boy/girl (etc.) but tell me more about what you're like.'

When a few more colourful and descriptive statements, one per child, have been made, start to offer an additional complimentary element of your own, modelling both the kind of depth you seek, and what it is 'OK' to say. Elicit a few more answers. Lastly, compliment the class on their insight and self-knowledge, and offer some general observations about what the class is like (e.g. you are an enthusiastic class, often hard-working, sometimes a bit noisy, mostly healthy, and ready to learn as much as you can. You're a friendly bunch, and I find it very enjoyable and rewarding being your teacher).

Activity 1

Ask the class to be prepared for you to ask them about 'what they are like' with their relationships. What aspects of relationships could they think about before answering? (How we get on with people, who we like, and dislike, how we cope with arguments, how we support each other, how we end friendships, how we choose friends, how friends choose us! etc.) Help them to generate a list of aspects and note them down. Tell the class this is to be a checklist for their next task. Can they recall earlier work on relationships? Draw their attention to content covered in earlier lessons, and use their recollections to further refine the checklist.

Give out activity sheet 1 and explain that it is for them to draw and write a 'thumbnail sketch' of 'What I am like with relationships'. Ask them to suggest the meaning of thumbnail sketch, explaining if necessary the brevity and speed implied by the term. Ask them to draw a speed picture of themselves, just head and shoulders, in the centre of the page. Then in the boxes, invite them to write statements starting with 'I...' which help build up a thumbnail sketch of them and relationships. Though not a hard-and-fast rule, each box is for a single topic on the checklist. Encourage them to talk to others if they aren't sure how they are seen or whether their view of themselves is in accordance with the perspective of those around them. Try to ensure they write some positive statements, though areas where development may be needed (managing anger, listening, making new friends, etc.) may be usefully recorded, too.

I am good at listening to my friends. I try to make sure they are happy and they don't get cross with me.

I try not to argue when someone disagrees with me because they have a right to their view. I try not to upset anyone.

I don't have many friends and I don't think I am good at making friends. I try to keep the ones I have.

I know to help if I can, and to ask someone if I am worried about a friend.

I get on well with Mum but Dad is harder. When he doesn't have time to listen to me I go and talk to my dog or kick a football.

This is what I'm like with relationships

Extension

If the exercise has been enthusiastically done and seems to tempt further work, invite everyone to choose one or two boxes to expand into a more detailed sketch of the topic it relates to. If one, insist it be predominantly a positive summary, one that details strengths. If a second is to be attempted, allow choice about whether to focus on an area of strength or one indicating developmental need or low confidence. Can needs be turned into targets? Give follow-up support to any child seeming to need it.

29 **The sort of person I am:** What am I like?

Ask everyone to reflect on how they relate to both sexes. How do they get on with girls, Mum or female carer, women teachers, female siblings, other female friends? Are the answers given by the boys in the class different from the answers given by the girls? How do both sexes expect this to be in future years? (The same? To change? If so, in what ways?)

Swap the focus to relationships with (and views of) males, asking mirror images of the same questions. You may want to give time for discussion in pairs before asking for feedback. Either way, encourage some class discussion and analysis of what emerges. Is the picture that has emerged predictable? What the children expected? What (if anything) are the surprises to them? Can they explain these surprises? Were the male and female questions and answers mirror images of each other (indicating similarity between the boys and the girls) or were they different? If different, why do they think this might be? Might this change in a year's time? Five years? Ten? Probe what they think and why, exploring varying views, but without making your own predictions – allow their present views to speak for themselves.

Be sensitive to the presence of emerging (rudimentary?) attractions, which will later gravitate predominately either to the same sex or to the opposite sex. Though your main task is to draw out the views of the children, avoid colluding with assumptions that heterosexuality is universal in your class. Judge sensitively whether the issues of sexual attraction and orientation are to be encouraged, explored, or simply allowed to rest if raised by a child. In any event it is OK to state that some people develop attractions to the same sex, others are attracted to the opposite sex, and some may find a mixture fascinating! If reassurance is needed, assure the class that some people's feelings change and grow at different rates, much like bodies. Wherever they've got to by now is OK, even if it means they aren't attracted to anyone!

Extension

Is there a way in which the 'findings' from this lesson can be graphically or pictorially represented? Can the children think how this might be done, and what its value might be? Remind them some people understand information more easily if they can see it. Could they collect the data more precisely from the class and input it to the computer to show what they have found out? They could discuss this with others, and ideas could be scribbled on activity sheet 2.

Reflect and act

Remind the children that they have come a long way since they were infants. They have many social skills and are able to make and manage friendships and relationships with a range of people, including some older or younger than themselves. They know what they like and admire in others, and what sort of friends they value. They are truly growing up.

Lesson 29

Activity Sheet I

What I'm like!

Draw a speed picture of your head and shoulders in the middle of the page. Round it, in the boxes, write short sentences that contribute to a thumbnail sketch of what you are like with relationships. Start each sentence with 'I ...'. Use the class checklist to remind you of the sort of things to think about.

This is what I'm like with relationships

(turn over and draw more boxes to write in if you need to.)

Names _____ **Date** _____

_____

_____

(Lesson 29)
(Activity Sheet 2) *Data input!*

Talk to those around you, and see if you can think of some ways to show what you have found out about how the sexes get on with each other. Can you use graphs? Or pictograms? Or pictographs? Or is there another way? Can you use the computer, or is it better to use paper and draw and write what you have found out? You will also need to find a way to get some definite data to show. How could you collect this?

To illustrate what we found out, we could

We think it is worth presenting this data because...

....

....

Sensitive issues 4 – Transition to Key Stage 3

(27) Transition to secondary or upper school

Secondary!

Preparation/materials

activity sheets 1 (if needed) and 2 (one per group). In activity sheet 2, extension you are invited to show your formal and appreciative recognition of the achievements of your class and its members. It will need some thought!

Key words

transition
trepidation
anticipation
excitement

Skills

assessing the validity of fears;
writing notes;
collecting information;
reviewing and celebrating achievement

Kick start

Ask the children to remember a time when they went to the dentist. How did they get there? How long did the journey take – was it at school or did they have to visit the dentist's surgery?

Did they have to sit and wait? What were they thinking? How were they feeling? Was the dentist nice? Kind? A good dentist? How did they feel after it was all over and they were home again?

Activity 1

Invite the children to think about the secondary or upper school they will go to. (Perhaps they aren't all going to the same one. Perhaps they call it the 'big school' or call each by name.) A little like visiting the dentist, there may be some uncertainty about what to expect.

Invite the children to have a brief chat with those sitting close to them, to consider the question 'In what ways is looking ahead to the big school like waiting for a dental appointment?' Stress that there are differences, but you are asking about the similarities. After a couple of minutes, seek feedback. The exercise may have been coloured by their experiences with dentists, but ask yourself if they seem to be nervous. Is there trepidation? Might there be particular fears you could help them explore?

Tell the class that you want to help them explore their ideas and feelings about what lies ahead, and that you will return to their more positive and excited feelings later on. First, though, ask them to tell you what they think might be strange to start with? What might be hard for them? What do they think might go wrong ? Judge the mood of the class, and how 'OK' they appear about expressing themselves openly. Could this be more appropriate as a written task? (activity sheet 1 is there, in case.) Or with ideas expressed on slips of paper given to you and dealt with one by one, preserving children's anonymity? Whatever format you pursue, respond to what they present, reassuring them where you can, but without criticising their feelings. Express empathy where suitable. 'I can hear you're worried about making new friends. It can take time. Anyone else feel worried about the same thing? Don't forget, the children you haven't met before may be just as worried about meeting *you*. You may be able to use *your* skills to help *them* feel more comfortable. How could you do that?' Some of their fears may be justified and unavoidable. (Further to travel, other children will be bigger, more homework, some friends won't be at the same school any more, etc.) Empathise. Be ready to gently challenge anything that is wrong, or too unlikely to be given house-room!

Is anyone worried about the *journey* to their new school? Explore this. Might a map help? www.multimap.com provides maps with a range of scales. www.youngtransnet.org.uk offers support and information to young internet surfers about making routes to school safer.

Is anyone concerned about being pressured to take illegal drugs by bigger children? This is a common fear, seldom borne out in fact. Opportunities, including offers, may become more plentiful as the children grow, but pressure from someone offering is unlikely. Research shows most who don't want drugs refuse successfully, and pressure is **not** usually a significant factor in determining drug-taking behaviour. Ask what they could do if unwanted offers worried them, and reassure them it's OK to talk to a new teacher about **any** worries they have.

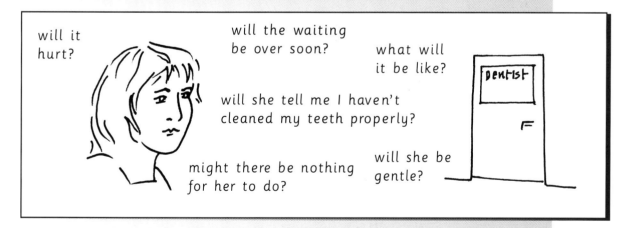

Extension

Turn the task round, and ask the children to tell you what excites them about going to secondary school. What are their hopes? What good things do they anticipate? What are they looking forward to? Give everyone a chance to think, and to answer if they want to.

Activity 2

Ask the children to think what they were like when they first went to school. How tall were they? How fast could they run? Could they ride a bike? What else can they do now that they couldn't then? (There should be lots of answers to this one, from sums to swimming and from seeking information to recognising and coping with emotions.) How much responsibility can they carry now? How much more are they trusted to do things for themselves? For others? How much more do they understand? You could use the example of the 'Key Words' aspect of this book's lessons and the class Circle of Feelings to start their answers to this question, together with the lessons' content – rights, campaigning procedures, etc. Their own examples could doubtless fill pages!

Can the children tell you some of their achievements? Take some declarations. Show your appreciation of their triumphs and accomplishments. Can they suggest achievements that belong *to the class*? Give them a chance to think about this, perhaps talking with others, before accepting feedback. List their ideas on the board or chart. Tell them you want to find a way of celebrating the progress and achievements of the class and its members, in such a way that they remind themselves how far they have come and find a way to present this to others. Ask them to discuss this idea in groups, concentrating on strategies and methods, not content, at this point. (An assembly, a play, a narration, a display of work, a giant poster, a frieze, a website, a newspaper with glowing headlines and written 'stories', a combination, etc.) Take their feedback and discuss as a class how this might best be done, and who the 'audience' might be . You might now divide responsibilities, giving some groups the task of 'collecting' individual and class achievement details and the others the task of refining the presentation plans. Activity sheet 2 can be used as a note pad.

When it's ready – let them do it! Praise their efforts. Support their ideas for sharing their achievements to a wider audience (other classes, teachers, parents). Help them turn it into a memorable celebration.

Extension

Reflect upon and prepare a way of showing your appreciation of the progress, the achievements and the quality of the class and everyone in it. Make it count! If you can, make it a surprise. (A little present for everyone? An outing? Photographs?)

Reflect and act

Did anyone ask their teacher 'Can I come back and see you?' Remind the children that they will be welcome to return and share their experiences of their new school with their 'old' teacher – just as long as they don't disrupt the work of their 'old' school. Suggest they talk to you later about when visits would be most convenient. And let them know you wish them good luck in their new school!

Lesson 30
Activity Sheet | *Big School!*

Draw a speed picture of your new school. Think how you feel about your new school. Can you make it have a face? Can you give the face an expression that fits? If the school seems friendly, give it a smile. Or does it seem a fierce school? Add some colour. Does it seem a brightly coloured school, or dark and gloomy? Write some words round it to describe the school and how you feel about it.

Write any worries or fears you have about going to the big school.

....

....

....

....

Secondary!
Real Health for Real Lives © Adrian King, Noreen Wetton, Nelson Thornes Ltd 2003

Names _____ **Date** _____

_____

_____

Lesson 30
Activity Sheet 2 — *Celebration time!*

This is a note pad. (Remember: this means you don't have to write whole sentences!) You will either be given Task A or Task B.
Task A is to collect as much information as you can about the achievements of the class as a whole, and of individual members.
Try to be fair to **everyone**.
Task B is to plan ways to present and celebrate the achievements of your class and its members. (Think: who will be the audience?)

Our notes

....

....

....

....

....

....

....

....

....

....

....

....

....

....